Destun Harris 2024 July

"I'm not usually a reader of memoirs or poetry, but I found this memoir stimulating to refl... ... and don't easily think o... ...rnt out, and came to liv... ...ave wondered how I wo... ...n is that of a profound th... ...God."

—**John Goldingay**, Fuller Theological Seminary (emeritus)

"Not only is Richard Bauckham a world-class scholar and a poet of wisdom and subtlety, but—as demonstrated here—it seems he can write of a 'difficult journey with God' in a way that puts him alongside some of the great spiritual writers of the past. Weaving together autobiography, poetry, and biblical and theological reflections, _The Blurred Cross_ has all the makings of a fresh Christian classic. You will finish the book profoundly grateful, not only to Bauckham for having written it, but even more, to the God who so obviously inspired it."

—**Jeremy Begbie**, Duke Divinity School

"Bauckham takes us on a remarkable journey along the anxious path of his failing eyesight. He leads us to a vista where God's providential care illuminates the experience of grace in weakness and results in the call to a life of thanksgiving. The book is striking in its vulnerability and clarity, as it weaves together the warp of human experience with the weft of scriptural study, theological reflection, and poetical imagination. The result is a rich tapestry that displays God's loving care, to encourage and challenge anyone who reads."

—**Elizabeth E. Shively**, George W. Truett Theological Seminary, Baylor University

"It is rare that a book by a scholar evokes a longing for a deeper faith, but in sharing his brush with blindness, Bauckham models the fruit of a lifetime of faithfulness. This book is more than an autobiography, although not less, as Bauckham focuses on a specific few months and weeks of deep fear in 2022. Bringing to his story the full weight of his immense intellect and literary depth, and sharing his own poetry and prayers, he gives a deeply personal account of seeing God's faithfulness, even in the 'coincidences,' and brings encouragement that testing is not in vain."

—**Mariam Kamell Kovalishyn**, Regent College

The Blurred Cross

A WRITER'S DIFFICULT JOURNEY WITH GOD

Richard Bauckham

Ⓑ
Baker Academic
a division of Baker Publishing Group
Grand Rapids, Michigan

Published by Baker Academic
a division of Baker Publishing Group
Grand Rapids, Michigan
BakerAcademic.com

Printed in the United States of America

Library of Congress Cataloging-in-Publication Data
Names: Bauckham, Richard, author.
Title: The blurred cross : a writer's difficult journey with God / Richard Bauckham.
Description: Grand Rapids, Michigan : Baker Academic, a division of Baker
    Publishing Group, 2024. | Includes bibliographical references and index.
Identifiers: LCCN 2023050980 | ISBN 9781540967435 (paperback) | ISBN
    9781540967718 (casebound) | ISBN 9781493445905 (ebook) | ISBN
    9781493445912 (pdf)
Subjects: LCSH: Perseverance (Ethics)—Biblical teaching. | Resilience (Personality
    trait)—Biblical teaching. | Spiritual life—Biblical teaching. | Spiritual
    life—Christianity.
Classification: LCC BV4647.P45 B38 2024 | DDC 231/.5—dc23/eng/20240116
LC record available at https://lccn.loc.gov/2023050980

24   25   26   27   28   29   30   7   6   5   4   3   2   1

To Jim Bennett
(1947–2023)
Best of friends

Contents

Preface

This book is about a period of less than three months in the spring of 2022, when I encountered and came through a critical experience. My eyesight deteriorated to the point at which I thought I might lose the ability to read or at least that reading would become very difficult. One of my eyes had become useless for reading six years previously, and now it seemed like the same might happen to my other eye. Thankfully, although I sustained some permanent damage to my eyesight, I am still able to read. But for someone like myself, for whom reading had been since childhood a virtually daily experience, and who remained committed to a life of study and writing that I understood to be my vocation from God, this was a very difficult time. Some people might call my experience a spiritual journey. I prefer to call it a journey with God. If the story is worth recounting, it is because I took every step of the way in a close relationship with God. It was one of the periods of my life in which I came closest to God. I am still reflecting on how I understand God's purpose for me and how I may live in a way that reflects my overwhelming sense of gratitude to God.

For readers to understand my experience, they need to know something about me and my life up to that point. Three chapters (2–4) provide that background. They are not intended to give even a sketch of my life as a whole. They simply pick out aspects of my life and experience that are relevant to the story I have to tell. As well as the narrative about myself, my eyesight, and God during those weeks in March–May 2022, I have included some extended reflections on issues arising out of the story. I have also included generous amounts of my own poetry, especially poems I wrote during that period or after it, when I felt strongly the impact it had on me. Some things are best expressed in poetry.

The book is an unusual mixture of autobiographical narrative, theological and biblical reflections, and poetry. I have written nothing in the least like it before. My hope is that this mixture helps me share something of value with readers. Each of us is unique. God made us so and loves us in our very uniqueness. Our walk with God, though we share much of it with others, is for each of us uniquely our own. All I have done in this book is to tell and reflect on a portion of my own story. How far it will chime with the experiences of my readers I can only guess. But I think the sharing of our experiences is a way of helping each other, in the words of my sainted namesake of Chichester, to know Jesus more clearly, love him more dearly, and follow him more nearly.

I am deeply grateful to many people who helped, encouraged, and prayed for me during the events I narrate. Some of them appear in my narrative; others do not. They are too many to name. When I tentatively began writing this book, Debbie Whitton-Spriggs and Jeremy Whitton-Spriggs each read two chapters and encouraged me to continue. Jim Bennett read the whole book chapter by chapter as I wrote it. I especially valued his reassurance that even though so many people encounter much more serious difficulties and obstacles in life, it was helpful for me to tell my story. He himself was diagnosed with myeloma around the same time as the events central to the narrative of this book. He died before the book was published, but I am glad he not only read it but also knew that I was going to dedicate it to him. I miss him very much and I am deeply thankful that I knew him.

1

A Memory of Tobit

It has not turned out as I expected,
but you have dealt with us according to your great mercy.

—Tobit 8:16

M y earliest memory of a stage play that told a scriptural story is not, as you might expect, of a nativity play. There must have been nativity plays performed at Downhills School in Tottenham, London, which I attended up to the age of seven, but I cannot remember them at all. Instead, I remember a play based on the book of Tobit. Tobit is a book that Protestants place among the Apocrypha because it is not in the Hebrew canon of Scripture, whereas for Roman Catholic and Orthodox Christians it is part of the Old Testament and sometimes called one of the deuterocanonical books. Canonical or not, Tobit is a delightful work of ancient Jewish literature. It has influenced the European artistic tradition, not least the work of Rembrandt. Some readers will know Salley Vickers's novel

Miss Garnet's Angel (2013), which creates connections between the story of Tobit and the modern narrative of the novel. (But readers of the novel should know that its summaries of the story of Tobit are no substitute for reading the book of Tobit itself.)

In the book, Tobit is an Israelite exile, living among the exiles from the northern kingdom of Israel in Nineveh, capital of the Assyrian Empire, with his wife and son, Tobias. He is known for his charitable deeds, but in the course of one of them, at the age of sixty-two, he loses his sight. He is burying a fellow countryman when bird droppings fall on his eyes and he becomes totally blind. He cannot work, and the family's situation becomes precarious. So he sends Tobias on a long journey to relatives in Media, with the aim of both finding a wife and collecting some money belonging to Tobit's family. Tobit hires a traveling companion for his son, who, unknown to them, is the angel Raphael disguised as a man. In the course of their journey, Tobias, under Raphael's guidance, catches a fish whose inner organs have medicinal properties. One of these is the gall, with which on his return Tobias is able to heal his father's eyes. (The rest of the story of Tobias's adventures need not concern us here.)

Although in the book Tobit himself is really the main character, in any dramatic version of the story, it is inevitable that Tobias should take that place. That seems to have been true of the play in which I acted, around the age of six. Of course, I knew nothing about the book of Tobit except the story as our class teacher told it to us. I do not know whether the play was her own adaptation of the biblical book or taken from a source. What I remember first is the way she cast the play by asking for volunteers to play each of the characters. She evidently wanted me to play the part of Tobias, but for some reason I did not want to. I think perhaps I did not want to be the child the teacher thought would best perform the central character. But instead I opted to play Tobit, the blind old man.

About the performance I remember only two things. One is that the teacher herself played the role of God. The curtains were parted just a chink so that she could be glimpsed, dressed in a white robe, and her voice be heard. It occurs to me now that a woman playing the part of God would be somewhat unexpected at that time. But we children did not think so. It must have seemed to us quite appropriate for the teacher to take the role of God.

My other memory is of sitting on stage on a chair. Tobit's was a rather static role, because he was completely blind and could not leave his chair without being led. I think he must have got up to greet his son on his return, as he does in the book, but I do not remember that. Nor do I remember Tobias's application of the fish's gall to heal Tobit's eyes. I just remember sitting there on the chair.

At one point in the course of the story I am going to tell in this book, I brought this early memory to mind. It seemed to me remarkable that as a young child I had played the part of a blind old man and now, an old man myself, I was suffering serious loss of sight. I was never in danger of becoming blind, as Tobit did, but the danger of losing all ability to read seemed to me a very real one at that point. For me, as I shall explain, losing the ability to read would have been massively life-changing. I was truly afraid of it. At that point I wondered whether these two experiences, seventy years apart, had a more than accidental connection. Might my eyesight be healed, as Tobit's was? I did not let that idea linger long in my mind, but it was an enticing one.

It is worth pointing out that in the story Tobit's healing is not miraculous in the strongest sense. The fish's gall had the medicinal capacity to heal the kind of blindness Tobit suffered

from. Where God's care and provision for Tobit came in was
in Raphael's role. Tobias would not have caught the fish or
known about the medicinal value of its internal organs had not
Raphael guided him and explained that to him. There are no
miracles in my story, at least not in the sense of scientifically
inexplicable events. Nor was my condition reversed in the way
Tobit's blindness was. But my childhood memory does seem
to me to prefigure my recent experience. Whether or not the
relationship is purely coincidental hardly matters to me. In any
case, it directs my attention with thanksgiving to God's presence in my story.

As an adult and a biblical scholar, I have returned to the
story of Tobit many times, even publishing an academic article
about the book of Tobit. But most recently I was reminded
of it near the beginning of the pandemic, just before the first
lockdown, when I visited the *Young Rembrandt* exhibition at
the Ashmolean Museum in Oxford. (It was to be the last time I
traveled outside Cambridge for more than a year.) Rembrandt
did many paintings and drawings of scenes from the book of
Tobit, mostly of Tobit himself. (It has been argued that he
was drawn to the figure of Tobit because his own father was
blind.)[1] It is natural to think of blind Tobit seated in a chair,
but for me that specific image from my childhood has been
reinforced by looking at those depictions by Rembrandt. In
his two finest paintings of Tobit,[2] Tobit is blind and seated,
a venerable and devout figure, depicted with notable empathy and affection. These associations led me to write this
poem:

1. Richard Verdi, *Rembrandt's Themes: Life into Art* (New Haven: Yale University Press, 2014), 143–46.
2. *Anna Accused by Tobit of Stealing the Kid* and *Anna and the Blind Tobit*.

BLIND TOBIT

In this chair
he has aged,
white-haired,
his life quelled and quieted
by patient waiting.

His face, at rest
as though dreaming
of another life,
is focused inwardly
on his God's patience
with his errant people,
exiled and waiting.

He hears the dog first,
clarion of the return.
Stirred from his stillness,
eager to see, though sightless,
he stumbles to the door.

Beyond expectation
comes healing.
Eyes filled with tears of joy,
mouth with praise of God.

Expecting his son,
he has waited also for God.
With opened eyes
he sees God's messenger
and in farsighted vision
God's future for his people.

Thus blessings overflow:
blessing of the Father
(the return of sight),
blessing of the Son
(the return with a bride),

blessing of the Spirit of prophecy
(the return of the people assured).

Associating my six-year-old self with this venerable figure
is incongruous. But associating my now much older self with
Tobit would also seem incongruous to me, because Tobit surely
is an *old* man. Though chronologically a little older than Tobit, I
really am not in the habit of thinking of myself as an "old man."
Admittedly, my beard would be white like Tobit's (according to
Rembrandt) if I grew it, but I do not, for that reason. But didn't
people age more quickly back then in biblical times? Yet I am
well enough aware that at seventy-six I can hardly pretend to be
middle-aged. What is it about old age that makes me reluctant
to put myself in such a category?

Michael Mayne, in his autobiographical reflections on old
age, written when he was about the age I am now, distinguishes
two aspects of old age: diminishment and gains.[3] If we focus on
the former, we see the later stages of life as a downward trajectory toward death. Famously, the speech Shakespeare attributes
to the melancholic character Jacques in *As You Like It* depicts
seven ages of life as the various parts that humans play on the
stage of the world. Old age comprises two ages.

> The sixth age shifts
> Into the lean and slipper'd pantaloon,
> With spectacles on nose, and pouch on side,
> His youthful hose well sav'd, a world too wide,
> For his shrunk shank, and his big manly voice,
> Turning again towards childish treble, pipes
> And whistles in his sound. Last scene of all,

3. Michael Mayne, *The Enduring Melody* (London: Darton, Longman &
Todd, 2006), 22–32.

> That ends this strange eventful history,
> Is second childishness and mere oblivion,
> Sans teeth, sans eyes, sans taste, sans everything.[4]

It would be difficult to imagine a sadder portrayal of senile decline. There is none of the respect for the old, as repositories of long and hard-earned wisdom, that is usually said to be characteristic of premodern societies. (It was not absent in Shakespeare's time, but it would have been out of place in this depiction of how actors play such parts.) The decline evident in the sixth age seems to be purely physical. On the stage such a character could be played for laughs. But in the "last scene" there is both mental and physical degeneration: second childhood, chronic loss of memory, and loss of key physical functions, including sight.

The difference modern medicine has made may be illustrated by the fact that the story I tell in this book concerns my eyesight, but at the same time as I was fearful of losing all ability to read, I was also in the final stages of having a tooth implant. To the dentist who performed it, I remarked that I wished he could do eye implants. (Perhaps one day that will be possible.) Degeneration of the eyes remains a challenge for medicine. My own experience heightened my awareness of how common it is for people in later life to suffer serious impairment of their sight. Eyes wear out, and the wear and tear cannot be so easily repaired as decaying teeth or arthritic hips. Really worthwhile advances have been made. Not so long ago, the degeneration of the macula that has occurred in both my eyes would have deprived me of all ability to read. As this story will tell, the treatment currently available saved much of my central vision in one eye. But research to find effective

4. William Shakespeare, *As You Like It*, act 2, scene 7.

treatments of macular degeneration is much needed and is ongoing.

Medical advances, together with economic resources, have enabled people in the affluent West to live, on average, much longer than Shakespeare's contemporaries did. Very often this means that they live with more or less serious physical impairments. Often very dependent on medical means to keep going and a good deal of physical assistance, they nevertheless live lives they find fulfilling and enjoyable. But longer life has also exposed far more people to the risk of serious mental deterioration, which Shakespeare calls "second childishness and mere oblivion" and we would call dementia. In addition, chronic loneliness afflicts many elderly people, living independently but housebound and unvisited. That can only rarely have happened in Shakespeare's England. All in all, while a contemporary description of the last two ages of humanity would differ considerably from Shakespeare's, someone as melancholic as Jacques would not find it difficult to paint just as gloomy a picture.

At seventy-six I am fortunate to have escaped so far most of the more serious effects of age. The threat to my eyesight that I describe in later chapters should be seen in that context. Nothing else was preventing me from working in the way that I had for the last fifteen years since I retired early from my university post. In a way, the opposite was the case. Freed from the seriously stressful conditions of work in a UK university, I felt more able to work well on the research and writing projects I had ahead of me. I am aware that getting older means I have less energy. (I think it was Peter Sellers who defined old age as when you bend down to tie your shoelaces and wonder if there is anything else you can usefully do while you're down there.) If I think back to a busy week during university term, when I was teaching undergraduates, supervising the work of at least a dozen doctoral students, and carrying out a demanding administrative role, I realize I would not now have the energy to do all those things. Teaching can be emotionally demanding in a way that research is not, for me at least, and now I have the freedom to vary my schedule at will.

I am certainly not aware of any cognitive decline, even though, like everyone else, I have been losing brain cells since my twenties. Of course, I forget names. Sometimes I go upstairs and forget why I came up. Yesterday I made myself a cup of tea, cut a slice of cake, and dumped it not on the plate but in the teacup. But these things are nothing in comparison with the fact that since 2005 I have been doing some of the best of my academic work, work that requires the accumulation of knowledge and experiences in a variety of specialist fields that come only from a long career of active research and persistent inquiry. Ideas flow thick and fast. In respect to my academic work, I feel not in decline, still less on the brink of giving it up, but as though I'm approaching the sort of summit that is bound to reveal further summits beyond it.

Diminishment is one aspect of aging, and I am certainly not immune from it. But the other aspect, which Mayne calls gains, I think could be called maturity. If I and many of my contemporaries do not readily think of ourselves as "old," that is probably because we associate the word with physical and mental decline. We do not feel that we are on the steeply descending incline to "mere oblivion, / Sans teeth, sans eyes, sans taste, sans everything." (We reckon with the real possibility of serious or fatal illness but expect it more as an interruption than the destination to which the course of our lives is leading.) While we passed the point of physical maturity long ago, maturity of the mind takes a different course. It comes of life experience and accumulation of skills and knowledge. It is the wisdom with which the old used to be conventionally associated, even though there were always plenty of old fools

around too. In today's world, young people are less inclined
to heed the advice or the teaching of those who are "older and
wiser." This must be largely a result of the accelerating pace of
change in our society. The old easily appear out of touch and
out of date. Indeed, they can easily feel out of place in a world
where they no longer seem to know the rules or understand the
culture. But it may be that the wisdom of the old is still valuable
precisely because they remember a world where things were
different. They know that not everything younger people take
for granted needs to be taken for granted. However, that is not
what this book is about.

In my experience, people in their seventies or even eighties
often say they do not feel old. "Inside" they are still young. I
think this is more than just a refusal to admit or succumb to the
signs of aging. I wonder if it reflects the fact that, as we move
on in life, we do not just leave behind the earlier phases of our
lives. In a sense we are still the child or the middle-aged person. Those earlier phases of our identity go into the making of
our later identity. Moreover, we remember them, with a sense
of continuity of identity. In old age, life may well become less
hectic, fewer new experiences come along, and life is often lived
more slowly. Our inner sense of ourselves does not change so
much—until something really new and disturbing occurs, like
the death of someone who has shared much of our life or the
onset of a life-changing disease or disability.

I find very attractive Michael Mayne's suggestion that we
picture the course of a life not as a circle (emerging from nothingness and returning to nothingness) nor as a straight line
(along which we are continuously just leaving the past behind
and moving on) but as a spiral.

> I can . . . see my life as a slowly ascending *spiral*. For a spiral sug-
> gests a life where each new circle—each new year or decade—

still contains within it the make-up of the old, the feeling of familiarity, the octogenarian still aware of what it *felt* like to be the child, the lover, the parent he or she once was, and still displaying the same recognisable characteristics, but wiser now, shaped by life's knocks, able to say, "I have been here before and learned a thing or two." Looking back, we can begin to understand our own unique story and see that we have been moving in a spiral around a centre. At the centre of every circle there is a still point.[5]

The center, which Mayne also calls the still point, is God. I would like to think of my life as having always spiraled around God, its center. In a later chapter I shall take up that theme of the theocentricity of my life. It is one image. For me, an equally important image is the simple one of God with me, God accompanying me through all the experiences of life, including those I shall describe in this story. That image too will recur.

Yet another image is of God carrying us through life. In the prophecy of Isaiah, God addresses his people thus:

> Listen to me, O house of Jacob,
>   all the remnant of the house of Israel,
> who have been borne by me from your birth,
>   carried from the womb;
> even to your old age I am he,
>   even when you turn gray I will carry you.
> I have made, and I will bear;
>   I will carry and will save. (Isa. 46:3–4)

The image of Israel as an old person is unusual and striking. Elsewhere in the Hebrew Bible, Israel is God's son, sometimes a small child who needs to be carried in arms. Presumably, old

5. Mayne, *Enduring Melody*, 40.

age is understood here as a phase of life in which one becomes weak and dependent once again. In that society, the old and frail may actually have been carried from place to place in the arms of the younger and stronger. By referring to Israel's dependence on God in these two phases of life, the earliest and the last, the prophet implies that, in reality, Israel is always radically dependent on God. Transferring these words about Israel to ourselves as individuals, we could say that we are entirely dependent on God throughout our lives, but in old age we may become more aware of our need to be carried in the strong and loving arms of God.

***

"Old men ought to be explorers," T. S. Eliot famously wrote near the end of his almost unbearably dark poem "East Coker," which became the second of his *Four Quartets*.[6] He was writing in 1940, when he was fifty-two. He describes himself in the poem as "in the middle," alluding to the opening of Dante's *Divine Comedy*, where Dante situates himself in the middle of his life. But Eliot seems to position himself on the threshold of old age. Dante's "dark wood" is dark "not only in the middle of the way but all the way."[7] For Eliot, perhaps, the "middle" is not so much a chronological date as the point in his life from which he can see the rest as dark "all the way." Old age is a quality of outlook, which he has already acquired. He dismisses the "wisdom of old men,"[8] supposedly based on the accumulation of knowledge and experience over a lifetime. We can, he claims, hope to acquire only "the wisdom of humility."[9] So Eliot is al-

6. T. S. Eliot, *Collected Poems, 1909–1962* (London: Faber & Faber, 1974), 203.
7. Eliot, *Collected Poems*, 199.
8. Eliot, *Collected Poems*, 199.
9. Eliot, *Collected Poems*, 199.

ready the old man who has renounced the quest for the kind of knowledge that, acquired in time, is overtaken in time. What then is left for the man who, whatever his chronological age, has reached the point of disillusionment with the progressivist's confident view of life?

> Old men ought to be explorers
> Here or there does not matter
> We must be still and still moving
> Into another intensity
> For a further union, a deeper communion
> Through the dark cold and the empty desolation,
> The wave cry, the wind cry, the vast waters
> Of the petrel and the porpoise.[10]

He is talking about an exploration that goes downward rather than outward, that is intensive rather than extensive. This is a movement into a deeper experience of the love of God, for, as the lines immediately preceding these explain:

> Love is most nearly itself
> When here and now cease to matter.[11]

But this is no easily found moment of mindfulness or mystical ecstasy (which Eliot has explicitly ruled out in this poem). It lies on the far side of a kind of dispossession of the self that Eliot portrays in the bleak imagery that ends the poem. This inhuman seascape is presumably the territory that "old men" ought to explore.

In the story I tell in this book, I did not set out to explore and never understood myself as an explorer. I had a vocation

10. Eliot, *Collected Poems*, 203–4.
11. Eliot, *Collected Poems*, 203.

from God (a dimension of relationship with God that does not feature in Eliot's reflections in *Four Quartets*) and was intent on pursuing it. What happened, happened to me. But I do recognize in the experience something of what Eliot here calls "still moving / Into another intensity / For a further union, a deeper communion" with God. My life with God is not different in kind from before, but God has, through a difficult experience, led me deeper into his love. It would be melodramatic to describe that difficult experience as "the dark cold and the empty desolation." It was never that bad. But since each of us is unique, an experience can seem to each of us uniquely testing and difficult to face. The story is understandable only as my story. Perhaps in pondering the story now as I write it I am an "old man" exploring.

2

"Always Reading"

Why are we reading if not in hope of beauty laid bare, life heightened and its deepest mystery probed? . . . Why are we reading if not in hope that the writer will magnify and dramatize our days, will illuminate and inspire us with wisdom, courage, and the possibility of meaningfulness, and will press upon our minds the deepest mysteries, so we may feel again their majesty and power?

—Annie Dillard, *The Writing Life*

There cannot be many people for whom reading is more important than it is for me. Since childhood the pleasure, as well as the utility, of reading has been a virtually daily experience. I recall a minor incident that occurred when I was a postgraduate student in Cambridge. I was lying on the sofa reading, as I often did, when the friend with whom I was sharing a flat came into the room. "You're always reading," he said. To him it seemed remarkable enough to call for comment. For me it seemed entirely natural that, whenever nothing else was happening, I should pick up a book. Nowadays many people pick up their phones whenever nothing else is happening (or even when something is), but my student days were long before mobile phones, emails, or the internet existed. I use the internet for email, information, and academic resources, but these have made little difference to the role of books in my life. I do not feel like one of a dying breed of people who read real books, because in fact more and more books are being published and bought.

There weren't many books at home when I was young, but my love of libraries began early. The Enfield Central Library had a children's library, an adult library, and a reference library. I remember I outgrew the children's library early and got special permission to use the adult library before, according to the rules, I was old enough. Much later I got to know and enjoy the reference library—an essential public amenity before the internet—and I often stopped off there for a while on my way home from school. Public libraries have changed so much that good bookshops are now more like libraries than libraries are. But I moved to Cambridge in retirement partly to be close to the best collection of academic libraries that there is for my interests. What I loved about the University Library, at least before the pandemic, was the sense of having immediate access to a vast world of books and journals. I loved not just the way this facilitated my work but the place itself.

My reading has by no means been limited to the fields of my academic specialisms. It is not all about work. I have been reading novels virtually all my life, if children's literature like the works of A. A. Milne, Enid Blyton, and Arthur Ransome can count as novels. By the age of seven I was even writing little storybooks of my own. As a child I read almost anything that happened to come to hand. I read the novel *Ben-Hur* by Lew Wallace years before the famous film was made in 1959. (The film somewhat disappointed me by leaving out stuff I really liked in the book.) I read the comic Doctor in the House novels of Richard Gordon merely because I found them in a house where we were staying on holiday. When we went on holiday in Dorset, I read Thomas Hardy, of course. These are random examples. By the time I left school, I had read all of Jane Austen, a particular favorite at that time.

During my six years as a university student, I read many of the great novelists of the twentieth century: Virginia Woolf, E. M. Forster, D. H. Lawrence, James Joyce, William Faulkner, Franz Kafka, Jean-Paul Sartre, and Albert Camus, among others. I read them for pleasure, but I also thought that the intellectual I aspired to be should be widely acquainted with modern literature. (I confess I read Joyce's *Ulysses*, without much enjoyment, because I saw it as an important novel. I never attempted *Finnegan's Wake*.) Of all these, the novels of Virginia Woolf and E. M. Forster are those I have gone back to from time to time throughout my life. If I had to pick one novel for a desert island, it might be Woolf's *To the Lighthouse*. In many cases, I can remember where I was when I read these novels (in various rooms and flats where I lived as a student, on a London underground train, in my bedroom at my family's home, in hotel rooms in Florence and Dublin). In periods when I was somewhat lonely, they were reliable and congenial companions.

In later years I read many more contemporary novels as well as classics of the past. For example, I read all twenty-six novels of Iris Murdoch, the later ones each year as they appeared with annual regularity. But I have never wanted to reread them. It would be tedious to catalog other novelists I have read, well over a hundred I would guess, but a few will illustrate the range: Penelope Fitzgerald, Shusaku Endo, William Golding, Amin Maalouf, Nadine Gordimer, Graham Greene, Jim Crace, George Mackay Brown, Julian Barnes, Henning Mankell, John le Carré, Ian McEwan, Robert Harris, Susan Hill. I cannot read popular fiction that is not well written. (I do not skim novels. I read every word, and so every word needs to be worth reading.) What I need is literary quality, compelling stories, characters with whom I can empathize, and insight into human life. I wonder what all this reading has done for me. Most of all, I think it has opened for me a vast range of human life and experience that could never have been available to me directly. C. S. Lewis spoke of "the enormous extension of our being which we owe to authors."[1] The best novels also accustom readers to recognize the profundity of life and to delve into it, not content to live superficially. No doubt this is why many of the best theological and religious writers read novels.

I should mention what my friends seem to regard as an amusing and rather perplexing eccentricity: my love of the Moomin books written and illustrated by the Finnish writer and artist Tove Jansson. I got to know the Moomin characters when they were available to English readers only in the brilliant cartoon strips published daily in the London *Evening News*. I still have a large collection of these strips that I cut out of the newspaper. (Only in recent years have they been published in book form.) I was already an adult when I read the books, beginning with *Comet in Moominland*, the first to be translated. I can see it now sitting on my bookshelf in my rooms at Clare College, where, I recall, it happened to sit alongside a history of Japan (a surprising, as I now see it, anticipation of my later interest in Japan, where the Moomin characters are greatly loved). Like all the best children's books, the Moomin books are full of insight as well as humor, which works for adults perhaps even better than for children. I have read them again and again. One of them will make an appearance in the story I tell in this book.

1. C. S. Lewis, *The Reading Life: The Joy of Seeing New Worlds through Others' Eyes*, ed. David C. Downing and Michael G. Maudlin (London: Collins, 2019), 8.

Novels have always been important to me, but so have poetry, biographies, and history. Over the years I have read philosophy, literary theory, political and cultural commentary, travel literature, art history, and natural history. Some of these books have had a connection with my academic teaching and writing; some have not. The boundaries between the two categories are fluid. If I'm interested in something, I read a book about it, and my interests are wide. Since my academic interests, teaching, and writing have ranged over historical theology, contemporary theology, biblical studies, ancient Judaism, contextual theology, and ecological ethics and theology, naturally all these areas are well represented among the books I possess. People ask, "Have you read all these books?" Of course not. I consult them, I read parts of them that matter to me, and sooner or later I need those that have stood untouched on the shelf for a long time. Finally, I should add that I have read many Christian books, not for their relevance to my academic work, but for their devotional and spiritual value for my own Christian life.

I love books and have a lot of them, but I am not a collector. In other words, I do not collect first editions or fine bindings. If a book is available in hardback and in a cheaper, paperback edition, I will always buy the latter. I love the content of books, not their superficial appearance.

I guess it must be true to say that all these books have made me who I am, just as much as the people who have influenced me and whatever other factors go into one's development as a human being over the course of a long life. Unlike some people, I cannot identify particular books that have changed my life or made a huge difference to it (other than the Bible, of course). So many books have made so many varied contributions to the way I think and live.

My aim in this chapter has been to give an impression of how indispensable books have been to me my whole life. Of course,

I have watched a lot of television, seen quite a few films (though far fewer than many of my friends), and enjoyed theater, art, and music, but at heart I am a literary person. Suppose I became unable to read? I hope I have given readers some sense of how massively life-changing that would have been. I hope you may even be able to understand how, even as I write this, thankfulness that it did not happen wells up in me. But more than that, having tried to summarize briefly what I owe to literally thousands of books, I am so grateful for those books. They have been among the greatest blessings of my life—and continue to be.

3

Writer and Scholar

My heart is inditing a good matter: I speak of the things which I have made touching the king: my tongue is the pen of a ready writer.

—Psalm 45:1 (KJV)

From an early age I knew I would write books. Of course, I had no idea that most of them would be theological books. (I didn't know there was such a thing as theology.) By the age of seven I was writing little stories as well as plays for my schoolmates to perform. That was when I overheard my mother talking to my father about her day and referring to me jokingly as "Shakespeare." I find it curious that I remember that. What did I know about Shakespeare at that age? I can't recall ever thinking of him as a role model. But getting back into one's mind as a young child is very difficult. I have so many fragments of memory but not much sense of what things meant to me.

When I was eight, we moved house. I sat on the stairs while the moving men emptied the house, recording what was happening in a small notebook. (I believe it still exists in a box of old family papers. My mother must have kept it.) Later, as a teenager at grammar school, I edited a magazine, composed entirely of humorous writing, which appeared every week during school term for several years and was known as *The Weekly Bish*. I hammered it out on my big, secondhand office typewriter, producing just two or three copies that were passed around the class at school. (Photocopying had not been invented.) There were several contributors, but I wrote most of it.

I don't remember seriously contemplating a career as a full-time writer. It would have seemed impractical. When I did think of a career, I envisaged nothing more ambitious than a teacher of history in a school, since history was my favorite subject. But I knew that somehow or other I would get to write books. Somewhere at the back of my mind, I think there was always the sense that my ideal life would be that of a full-time writer. Most of the many biographies I have read over the years have been of literary figures—novelists and poets, sometimes academics who are best known as writers.[1] So when in 2007 I retired from university employment in order to devote my time mainly to research and writing, I felt as though this was the part of my working life for which the rest had been preparing me. I have never seen it as retirement or even semiretirement, though advancing age has slowed me down a bit. I have no desire or need to stop working now that I am free to be just a scholar-writer.

The fact that I have always thought of myself as a writer or scholar-writer partly explains why researching and writing have

---

1. I am thinking of such figures as C. S. Lewis, J. R. R. Tolkien, and Iris Murdoch.

always been a priority for me, even when my other duties in university employment were sufficient for a full-time job and most other academics in that situation would not have got much writing done. People sometimes ask how I have managed to publish so much. One answer is "I'm a writer; it's who I am." Another is "It's my vocation from God." The latter aspect I shall defer until the next chapter. I do not wish to leave the impression that teaching has not been important to me. I taught in universities for three decades. My courses were popular, and I put a lot of work into them. I also supervised a large number of postgraduate students writing doctoral theses. All these students really mattered to me. Teaching also helped me become a better writer than I otherwise might have been. Engaging with a live audience is a great way to clarify both one's thinking and one's ways of communicating it. But for the story I have to tell, set in 2022, it is my vocation as a writer rather than a teacher that is relevant.

I have used the term *scholar-writer*. Most writers are not scholars, and many of those whose biographies I have mentioned were not, though some were. Scholars usually write articles and books, but I am not sure whether most of them think of themselves as writers. But in my case, the assumption that somehow or other I would write books came first. It was a natural assumption for someone who read as many books as I did and also did well in such writing exercises as school required of me. But in my early teenage years I also developed a deep love of historical research, which soon led me into biblical studies.

At my grammar school we started history back in the ancient Near East. I vaguely recall that we moved on via the Roman Empire to Anglo-Saxon England, after which history at school became English history. But I was fascinated by the ancient empires: the Assyrian, the Babylonian, and the

Persian. Perhaps I was attracted simply by their exotic other-
ness. In any case, I read what I could find in the library about
them, which included, as I recall, a book called *The Bible as
History*. Reading about the Persian Empire, I think I already
had a historian's instinct to want to grapple with the primary
sources, and the Old Testament offered some easily accessible texts of the period that I could study for myself (in the
King James Version!). So I acquired the International Critical
Commentary volume on the biblical books of Ezra and Nehe-
miah and somehow managed to cope with its very technical
discussions of the Hebrew text. At the same time I read the
Greek historian Herodotus on the Persian Wars and tried to
put the book of Esther together with Herodotus's account of
the Persian king Xerxes.

That was the beginning of my interest in both historical
research and biblical studies as academic pursuits. The former followed its own trajectory, leading me into the study of
history for my first degree at the University of Cambridge,
with a specialization in the Reformation period, and then to
a doctoral thesis about a sixteenth-century English theologian. Then theology itself became a major interest, and for
fifteen years I taught historical and contemporary theology
at the University of Manchester. I wrote about the work of
the contemporary German theologian Jürgen Moltmann and
developed some of my own theological thinking in dialogue
with his. But biblical studies also had a parallel trajectory in
my life, spurred on by the burgeoning of my own Christian
faith, in which the Bible was of key importance. So somehow
I became a scholar with a keen interest in Christian theology
and an unquenchable desire to study the Bible. My training in
history equipped me very well for the academic discipline of
New Testament studies, which has traditionally been a largely
historical enterprise. But I was always also concerned for the

theological relevance of the biblical texts today. In 1992 I became Professor of New Testament Studies at the University of St. Andrews in Scotland. On book jackets and the like I am sometimes described as one of the leading New Testament scholars in the world. As well as very specialist studies, I have written books that have reached a wide audience outside academia.

This book is not about my academic career, and so I am contenting myself with that very brief summary. But I want to return finally to my sense of myself as a writer, which I feel lies even more deeply in my sense of self than my many academic interests. I no longer aspire, if I ever did, to be another Shakespeare! But it has pleased me a great deal that my first collection of poetry was published in 2022.[2] I have written poetry throughout most of my life, but in the busy years of my career I often managed only my regular Christmas poem, expected by those friends who received one every Christmas. (I wonder if anyone else has written as many poems about the magi as I have.) Poetry requires a mood of receptivity that takes time, more time than the difficult task of actually writing a poem takes. So most of the poems in the collection were written in the last fifteen years. They doubtless owe much to the way the creative part of my mind has been formed by long years of reading poetry and other literature, as well as thinking about God and life. I do not think they owe much to my biblical scholarship. They belong to a different part of what being a writer means for me. They contribute to my sense that these later years of my life, those in which I have been free to be "just" a scholar-writer, are those for which the rest of my life had been preparing me.

2. Richard Bauckham, *Tumbling into Light: A Hundred Poems* (Norwich: Canterbury Press, 2022).

I mention my poetry here partly because some later chapters of this book contain poems that (with one exception) were written during or soon after the three months on which this book is focused. Some are among the most personal poems I have written. They, along with the commentary I provide, combine with the narrative to tell my story.

4

Vocation

Jesus calls us, o'er the tumult
of our life's wild, restless sea;
day by day his voice invites me,
saying "Christian, follow me!"

—Cecil Frances Alexander,
"Jesus Calls Us, O'er the Tumult"

B eing a Christian in practice is not just a matter of trying to
live a morally good life. Nor is it just a matter of going to
church. It is about dedicating one's whole life to the service of
God in following and in fellowship with Jesus Christ. I don't
know when it first dawned on me that this is what being a
Christian meant. I know I was well aware of it by the time I
left school, as anyone who studied the Bible and regularly attended worship, as I did, would be. I also know that I found
it profoundly attractive. What more wonderful thing could
there be to do with one's life than to dedicate it to the service

of God? What else could give such comprehensive meaning and purpose to life? Quite simply, I loved God and wanted to live for God.

I remember that during my first year as a student at Cambridge I read a book by Michael Griffiths called *Take My Life*.[1] I know it was during my first year in Cambridge because I remember reading it in the college rooms I lived in that year (M2, Memorial Court, Clare College). I do not remember much about the book except that it was based on the hymn by Frances Ridley Havergal. The first and last verses of the hymn are:

> Take my life and let it be
> consecrated, Lord, to thee.
> Take my moments and my days;
> let them flow in endless praise.

> Take my love; my Lord, I pour
> at thy feet its treasure store.
> Take myself, and I will be
> ever, only, all for thee.

During my student years I read quite a few Christian books, but the fact that I recall where I read this one suggests it was important for me. I resonated strongly with the theme of the hymn and the book.

I realize that this kind of religious commitment can appeal to young adults at a time when they are looking for direction for their lives. For some people it is an early enthusiasm that fades as other things crowd into their lives and seem to fill their lives quite adequately. Maybe in this respect I never grew up. In fact, I did a lot of growing up, some of it painful, in my early twenties, but my orientation to loving and serving God matured

1. Michael Griffiths, *Take My Life* (London: Inter-Varsity, 1967).

too. God remained the horizon against which everything else in my life played out. Fortunately, from an early stage, I knew that living for God would not always be easy.

I don't mean to suggest that this orientation of my life to God has been steady and unwavering throughout my life. It is true that I have never been much troubled by intellectual doubts. Already as a teenager I explored rather carefully the credibility of Christian faith. (C. S. Lewis, among others, was important in that exploration.) As a naturally intellectual person, I never really stopped thinking seriously about such matters and never found reason to doubt my early conviction that Christianity offered the most plausible basis I knew for finding meaning in life. I also learned how to live with questions because it would be unreasonable to expect that conclusive answers to all our questions about God and the world could be available to finite creatures like ourselves, with all our necessary limitations of knowledge and intelligence. Rather, if one were to treat Christian faith as a kind of hypothesis—and there are good intellectual grounds for at least entertaining it as a promising hypothesis—then it is in trying to live out Christian faith and practicing the presence of God in real life that the hypothesis receives ample confirmation. On the intellectual level, as a theologian I am familiar with most of the objections, such as those of the new atheists, and I know how to respond to them, which does not always mean answering them. Sometimes it makes good sense to defer answers. That is not the same as doubt.

While I have never found good intellectual reasons to doubt, neither have I encountered experiential ones. I know that some people lose their faith owing to the impact of suffering (I use that term to cover the wide range of sorrows and troubles

that come to people in life), but I also know that others come
through suffering with their faith deepened. I belong to this
latter group. In difficult times I come closer to God. I become
more aware of my need for God, and always I find God to
be with me, enfolding and sustaining me with his love. The
story I have to tell in this book will illustrate that. Other people's suffering is another matter and for me more perplexing
and painful to consider. There I have to defer any conclusive
answers.

Thus, doubting God has not been a problem in my life. I have
the feeling that from an early age my life has been so grounded
in God that only a great upheaval could shake that founda-
tion. I could not, as some people seem to do, lose sight of God
almost without noticing. On the contrary, I find life without
God almost unimaginable. I can see how people may feel satis-
fied with life without God if they have never known life with
God. But after knowing the incomparable depth and breadth of
meaning that knowing and loving God give to everything else
in life, I believe that losing faith and living without God would
surely be unendurable. So in those rare and transient moments
when the possibility that there is no God has seemed to me a
genuine possibility, it has felt like the opening of a bottomless
abyss of nihilism. Nietzsche is the postmodern prophet who
descended open-eyed into it and did his best to celebrate it. He
is a powerful antidote to the superficiality of the "new atheists,"
who seem able merely to wander along the edges of the abyss,
blithely unaware of it.

While the orientation of my life to God has not been seriously impeded by doubt, my faithful attention to God has undoubtedly wavered. Of course, I have yielded to distractions.
Of course, I have wandered from the way. There is much that
I remember with shame and regret. I can only thank the grace
of God that some genuine love of God has never actually left

me. The unknown medieval mystic who wrote *The Cloud of Unknowing* speaks of the "leash of longing," by which God never lets us stray too far from him before drawing us back.[2] In my experience, God is an irresistibly alluring presence, to which sooner or later I must always return.

The previous chapter and what I have written so far of this one together form the context for what I have to say about my vocation, an idea that will be prominent in the story at the heart of this book. A vocation (from the Latin *vocare*, "to call") is a calling. Originally it referred to being called by God to serve him, though in modern secular use the implication of a divine origin of the call has been lost. In Christian history the word has acquired some specific meanings: a vocation to the religious life (in a religious order) or a vocation to Christian ministry. In Reformation theology, every Christian's occupation was understood to be their vocation, and this usage underlies the modern secular usage, in which a vocation is an occupation or role to which one commits one's life (as a medical doctor, a nurse, an artist, a poet, a politician). Usually the implication is that this is not merely a job done to earn a living but something worth devoting one's life to, perhaps entailing sacrifice. It is in at least this sense that I speak of my vocation as being a writer-scholar, but I also intend the older sense of being called by God to this particular form of service to God.

In the New Testament, the predominant sense of calling is God's call to people to believe and to obey—that is, to be

---

2. *The Cloud of Unknowing*, chap. 1. Long ago I put this metaphor to my own use. The *Cloud* author used it to speak of the way God draws us onward to further stages of the spiritual life. I use it to mean that God's leash allows us some scope for straying but always draws us back to him.

Christians. Paul sometimes refers to Christians as those "called to be saints" (Rom. 1:7; 1 Cor. 1:2), where "saints" or "holy ones" means not, as modern usage tends to mean, people who live remarkably good lives but people who are dedicated to the service of God. Paul also says that they are "called to belong to Jesus Christ" (Rom. 1:6). He begs them "to lead a life worthy of the calling to which you have been called" (Eph. 4:1). But there are also cases in which a calling is a specific form of service to God. Paul speaks of himself as "called to be an apostle" (Rom. 1:1; 1 Cor. 1:1); he also perhaps speaks of the states of marriage and celibacy in terms of how different Christians are called to live (1 Cor. 7:17).

It is the vocation of all Christians to be friends and followers of Jesus, to be children of God, and as such to love and to serve God. Within that overall calling to live our whole lives in the service of God, there may be specific tasks and roles to which we are called. For example, we may be called to a specific profession or line of work, to marriage, to parenthood, to voluntary service of many kinds, to friendship, and so on. As commitments, some of these may be lifelong, some time-limited. Some will require major resources of time and energy, some much less. All are ways of loving God and our neighbors. Some we may feel to be so important as to contribute to our sense of identity, of who we are, though in this respect they must be less important than our fundamental identity as those who belong to Jesus Christ. Paul's sense of calling to be the apostle to the gentiles encompassed his whole life, as few other callings do, but for all that he was even more fundamentally a Christian who regarded his fellow Christians as brothers and sisters. After death he would lay down his apostolic commission but remain God's beloved child.

Readers of the previous chapter and this one will not be surprised that I see my role as writer-scholar as my vocation (and at this point I include also teacher as part of the same vocation). It does not encompass my whole life, because my life extends to other roles in the church community, among friends, and in the wider community. Above all, my relationship with God goes much deeper and wider than this specific vocation. But I have certainly devoted much more of my life to it than most people do to an occupation. When I had my first teaching post in a university department of theology—which I regarded as a great privilege and responsibility—I was disappointed to realize that for some of my colleagues it was much more like an ordinary job. For me, being a theologian was something to devote my life to, and I thought myself fortunate to have a "job" that I felt was worth that kind of dedication—one that was endlessly interesting as well. The duties a university teaching and research post requires are fairly open-ended: one should do research and write, but no one can put a limit on that; good teachers put more time into preparation than others; one may or may not attend conferences; and for most of my career, no one thought of calculating the hours one was working for the salary received. (In my view, that situation enabled universities to exploit their academic staff.) But in my case my vocation always exceeded the requirements of the job. I took on all kinds of tasks and responsibilities additional to the job and worked excessively hard for most of my career. I never saw such things as ways of advancing my career. They were ways of fulfilling my vocation. Until I became ill from stress toward the end of my time at St. Andrews, I was willing to give as much as I could to serving God as a writer-scholar-teacher. But I should also say that I got enormous pleasure from study and research, pursuing matters of absorbing interest to me. Genuine service combines duty and delight but requires also that one keep going in times of difficulty.

I have sometimes thought my dedication to being a writer-scholar-teacher of theology and biblical studies resembles the total life commitment of a monk. One big difference, however, is that a monk commits to lifelong disciplines. For me, flexibility and lack of order have always been a way of life. I recall once telling a friend that I never kept much chocolate in the house because otherwise I would not be able to resist eating it all. He said he was surprised that such a self-disciplined person as me would have that problem. I suppose he thought I must be very disciplined to have done all the work that I have. But I have never thought of myself as disciplined. What I have, I think, is not discipline but drive. When and how I get things done are quite haphazard. I never achieve all that I mean to in a week, a month, or a year. I meet deadlines for live events (a lecture to be delivered next week) but not the deadlines I set myself (and promise to publishers) for books. I start new projects without finishing others.

Since retiring from my university post at St. Andrews, of course my life has become even more haphazard. Whether I shall be working and at what times of day is something I rarely know, unless I have commitments that exclude parts of the day from work. The disciplined days of most full-time writers—say, four hours of work before lunch, a two-hour walk in the afternoon, an hour for emails and such, evenings for social activities and relaxation—are completely alien to me. I make my haphazard way through the week, following my inclinations as they vary from day to day—meeting friends, taking walks, doing the household chores, shopping, watching television, reading—but also driven by my commitment to serve God in my vocation. When I can't seem to get down to work, there are other things to do. When work is going well, I can exploit that and work long hours. But not at the expense of sleep. No other time of the day is out of bounds for work, but my eight hours of sleep are sacrosanct. I cannot function properly without them.

My vocation itself is flexible in its content. It no longer includes academic teaching.[3] It has always included some preaching. In recent years it has come to include poetry. It now includes this book.

3. After moving to Cambridge, I taught some courses for ordinands at Ridley Hall and the Cambridge Theological Federation, but I retired from this role in 2020. I deliberately gave up all postgraduate supervision when I retired from St. Andrews University.

5

The Story, Part 1
The Blessings of Alnmouth

Take the shield of faith, with which you will be able to quench
all the flaming arrows of the evil one.

—Ephesians 6:16

M y story begins in March 2022, when we in the UK felt
that we were probably emerging from the Covid-19 pandemic. For two years we had lived with major restrictions on
our lives, though the rules varied and were at some times more
restrictive than at others. There had been nothing else remotely
like the pandemic in our lifetimes. Comparisons were often
made with wartime, and there were some similarities (especially with the "home front") as well as obvious differences.
The pandemic was harder to endure for some people than for
others. Living in retirement with financial security, I knew my
own situation was privileged. The arrival of vaccines against

the virus made a huge difference. In time, far fewer people were taken into intensive care or died from the virus.

Two years after the beginning of the first lockdown, in March 2022, many restrictions had been lifted. We were returning, some more cautiously than others, to a semblance of "normal" life—life as it used to be, before the pandemic. On February 14 I took the train from Cambridge to London to see an exhibition of Van Gogh's self-portraits. It was not the first time I had seen an exhibition in London since before the pandemic, but it was the first time I traveled on the London Underground, generally considered one of the places where a person was most likely to catch Covid. I had had three doses of the vaccine and had also had Covid, very mildly, and so I felt fairly safe, but not without misgivings.

The period of the pandemic was a strange one in more ways than one. It was not only a very unusual time but also a time that affected our experience of time. For many people, life slowed down. It is a common observation that the years just before the pandemic seem very distant and it is hard to remember the chronological sequence of events in those years. I remember, for example, visits to give invited lectures in Rome, Lublin, Paris, and Sweden, but I cannot remember in what years or in what order they occurred. Time was different then. We were different too.

In a sermon I preached on the first Sunday of Lent (March 6, 2022), I made this suggestion:

> We could make this Lent a time for thinking about the way ahead—for ourselves as individuals and families and for ourselves as a church community. Let's open our hearts and minds to God's guidance for the way ahead. It's almost two years now from the beginning of the first lockdown. Some might say we have had two years of Lenten disciplines. It has been hard for

everyone, for some much more than others. And it will have changed us—in ways we may not yet be able to understand. It has changed our society and our church. The pandemic is not over, but the gravest dangers are past. It is time to get our bearings and orient ourselves to the future God has for us.

Good sermons are often preached to the preacher as well as to the hearers. In this case I decided I should set aside some time to think and pray about God's direction for my life, now that I was emerging from those two strange years of pandemic.

I had planned a short visit to St. Andrews in Scotland, where I have a holiday home, stopping on the way to spend a few days at the Franciscan friary in Alnmouth. Alnmouth is a village beautifully situated on the coast of Northumberland. It has a station conveniently located on the main East Coast railway line, and despite the small size of the village, a good many of the trains from London to Edinburgh stop there.

I had visited the friary just once previously, twenty years earlier, when I was living in St. Andrews. I had just finished writing a major book, *Jesus and the Eyewitnesses*. I had been working rather intensively on it and was very tired. I remember that at the friary I slept a lot. I don't remember much else except that a cat visited me in my room. I love cats, and perhaps I remember the cat because I was more fond of cats than of friars. Sadly, there are no cats at the friary now. On this second visit I did suggest that there should be, because stroking cats is therapeutic and some of their visitors would benefit. Furthermore, surely Franciscans should have animals around? The brothers thought maybe they should get a cat but also pointed out that there are a lot of birds there and even Franciscan cats are prone to catch birds.

The friary used to be a family home, a thirty-roomed mansion built early in the last century by a shipping magnate. He chose for it an ideal location, on high ground looking directly out to sea. The Franciscan brothers who now occupy the house offer hospitality to anyone wanting a quiet time for a few days. They sing regular services throughout the day that guests can attend as they choose. Guests are not allowed to use Wi-Fi in their rooms, and silence must be observed from 9:00 p.m. onward. Because it was Lent, there were some additional restrictions. Silence was to be maintained for the whole evening after supper, and supper itself was silent on two of the days I was there. I expected that silent supper would conform to the monastic practice of silent meals at which one brother would read aloud, but there was no reading. I found totally silent supper rather grim. Because I needed Wi-Fi to check my email, one evening I went to a pub in the village after supper and had a beer. (This was entirely within the rules for guests!) Food at the friary was plainer than usual because of Lent, but it was generally good, and I do not find good plain food a hardship. What I wanted was a few days for quiet reflection, with services to attend and meals provided.

On the day of my arrival, the weather had been good on the journey from Cambridge, but just as the train pulled into Alnmouth, there was a heavy shower of sleet. I missed the most direct route from the station to the village and arrived at the friary rather wet and cold. But the abundant spring flowers on the approach to the house were happily welcoming. When one of the brothers showed me to my room, I was surprised to find it was large, with twin beds, surely the largest of the guest rooms. But the best thing about it was that it had a wide bay window looking straight out to sea. There were even binoculars provided. The guest rooms are named after saints, and I noticed later that mine was "St. Louis." St. Louis was a medieval king of France. The room, I suppose, was the room most fit for a king.

The village itself was once a significant port, until the River Aln changed its course and the estuary became no longer navigable for any but the smallest boats. So it has historic buildings and attracts visitors in the holiday season. In March it was very quiet. On walks around it I got the impression that everyone who lives there must have a dog. Probably most also have golf clubs, and some have boats. The only coffee shop (actually called the "tea rooms") did not open until 10:30, and admission was by ringing the bell. But they had Wi-Fi. All this was conducive to peaceful reflection. One afternoon, when there was a very cold wind, I was content to enjoy the view from my window. In the evenings I could use the binoculars to view the lights out at sea and wonder what they were. Not far from my room, the library, always empty when I visited it, had an equally fine view. I had rather hoped to write a poem or two, but not even a few words of one dropped into my mind.

To my inquiry about God's direction for my life henceforth, the answer seemed very clear. I summed it up in one phrase: "keep on keeping on." (I borrowed the phrase from Alan Bennett, who used a version of it as the title of one of his volumes of diaries,[1] but I can't remember what he meant by it exactly. A quick search of the internet suggests that Bennett borrowed it from a song.) In other words, my vocation and the specific form it had taken in the fifteen years since I had retired from my chair at St. Andrews remained the same. Thinking about it before God, I could not see any reason for change. That I discerned God's will for me to be to continue to work on my major writing projects was to become very important in this little story because what happened subsequently was a real

1. Alan Bennett, *Keeping On Keeping On* (London: Faber & Faber, 2016).

challenge to that discernment. Could I continue such work if reading became very difficult for me?

In retrospect, my vocation to write important books has been the aspect of "keep on keeping on" that I have very often recalled. But what I wrote in my journal at the time shows that I also had other aspects of the direction of my life after the pandemic in view:

> The way ahead for me is clearly to keep on keeping on!
> Working hard. Keeping in touch with friends and caring about them. Keeping in close touch with God.
> Writing more poetry again?

The query at the end in part reflected the fact that I had written no poetry since Christmas, because I was determined to give all my attention to finishing my "pandemic project," my two-volume work on the expression "son of man." But I think it probably also reflected the fact that I had hoped my time in Alnmouth might produce a poem or two, but it had not done so.

It was also on the same day that I wrote this prayer in my journal: "Keep me from self-importance, self-promotion, and possessiveness." The greatest danger in a vocation is turning it from being for the glory of God to being a search for glory for oneself.

The next day I wrote, "Lord God, keep far from me all that would impair my ability to serve you." I think this thought was provoked by "St. Patrick's Breastplate," to which I must now turn.

I took with me to Alnmouth a booklet by Graham Pigott called *Prayers to Remember*.[2] It is about the value of memoriz-

2. Graham Pigott, *Prayers to Remember* (Cambridge: Grove, 1995).

ing a few really helpful and inspiring prayers, and I wanted to memorize two or three of the twelve that he selected as examples of such prayers. One that I did memorize was a verse from Mrs. Alexander's translation of the Old Irish hymn often known as "St. Patrick's Breastplate." It will be well known to many readers.

> Christ be with me, Christ within me,
> Christ behind me, Christ before me,
> Christ beside me, Christ to win me,
> Christ to comfort and restore me.
> Christ beneath me, Christ above me,
> Christ in quiet, Christ in danger,
> Christ in hearts of all that love me,
> Christ in mouth of friend and stranger.

Later I would repeat this prayer in difficult circumstances, such as when I was in the waiting room of the eye clinic at Addenbrooke's Hospital. I would also compose for my own use a substitute for the second half of it:

> Christ, embrace me,
> Christ, enfold me.
> In your great love
> firmly hold me.

Later still, I varied this to what I think is an improved version:

> Christ, embrace me,
> Christ, enfold me.
> Christ, with your strong
> love uphold me.

For the time being, however, I simply memorized the original version.

Many years ago I read David Adam's book of reflections on the whole of "St. Patrick's Breastplate" (nine verses). The book's title is the alternative title of the hymn: *The Cry of the Deer*.[3] Remembering that the book had been of some importance to me, I found a copy in the friary library. What it mainly did for me on this occasion was to remind me of the whole hymn. Adam provides both Mrs. Alexander's version, which is a good translation, and another translation from the Old Irish original. (Mrs. Alexander's version is printed in the appendix to this chapter.)

It so happened that the last of my three days at the friary was St. Patrick's Day (Thursday, March 17). At the midday mass the brothers sang all nine verses of "St. Patrick's Breastplate." It was a stirring performance. I was almost inclined to clap when they finished. The tunes to which they sang the hymn ("tunes" because the verse that begins "Christ be with me" requires a different tune from the other verses) were those commonly used. They are a peculiarly good match with the sentiments as well as the rhythm of the words. The powerful impact of this hymn derives from this combination of verbal meaning and music. Certainly I was deeply affected. I wrote in my journal that the "strength and vigor" of it affected me: "The hymn expresses above all *vigorous* faith, which is perhaps what I needed." At the beginning of the service I had actually asked God for a blessing of some kind. I think I had been a little disappointed that I had not been able to write a poem during my stay and had not

3. David Adam, *The Cry of the Deer: Meditations on the Hymn of St. Patrick* (London: SPCK, 1987).

received any fresh or significant insight. I wanted something to take away with me. So I felt that "St. Patrick's Breastplate," with its expression of vigorous faith, is what I had been given. When I wrote that vigorous faith was perhaps what I needed, I had no notion of the way in which that turned out to be very much what I needed to be given by God in the following weeks. The coincidence between the singing of this hymn and the fact that just previously I had adopted the eighth verse of the hymn as a prayer to memorize and use habitually was not, of course, lost on me. It was one of a series of "coincidences" that run through this story.

"St. Patrick's Breastplate" probably does not go back to Patrick himself (fifth century) but dates from the early eighth century. Its unique form and content (among Christian hymns) evidently reflect a pagan Irish tradition of incantations used as charms against enemies, human and demonic. In that respect it rather resembles Psalm 91, a text that ancient Jews and Christians used to place in amulets, to be worn on the person as protection against evil forces. But the Breastplate is nevertheless massively Christian, with its opening and closing invocation of God the Trinity. It invokes the power of this trinitarian God in five verses that evoke an extraordinary range of aspects and instances of the divine power to protect. First and foremost, it rehearses the story of Jesus from his incarnation to the future judgment, a kind of creedal summary of the events that established his power of salvation. Exceptional creatures, angelic and human, who embody divine power in their various roles, compose the next verse. The hymn then turns to the rest of creation, focusing on those features that manifest their Creator's power. Finally, verse 5 enumerates the attributes and qualities of God himself, which provide the speaker with not only powerful and timely protection but also direction and guidance, wise instruction, and inspired speech. All these arm the speaker against the

forces of evil that are vividly described in verses 6–7. There are
temptations and sinful tendencies within, all manner of human
enemies without, and a terrifying selection of the devil's many
wiles and devices.

What in all this struck me as "astonishing," as I wrote in my
journal, was "the unwavering confidence" of the speaker of the
hymn. It is not so much a prayer for protection as a confident
claim to protection, faithfully asserted against the very real
strength of ubiquitous adversaries. That is what I felt to be
"vigorous faith." Psalm 91 expresses rather similarly a conviction that those "who live in the shelter of the Most High" (v. 1)
can claim him as the refuge and fortress in which they may put
unwavering trust. The psalm assures them of divine protection
against all evils.[4]

But even more similar to the Breastplate is the remarkable
passage with which Paul concludes his Letter to the Ephesians,
urging his readers to "be strong in the Lord and in the strength
of his power. Put on the whole armor of God, so that you may
be able to stand against the wiles of the devil" (Eph. 6:10–11).
The author of the Breastplate imagines himself, as it were, don-
ning that armor of divine protection in the face of supernatural
as well as more ordinary enemies. But whereas Paul focuses
on what God gives believers with which they can ward off evil
(truth, righteousness, faith, and so on), the Breastplate invokes
the power of God itself in all its astonishing range of aspects
and manifestations.

I think that on St. Patrick's Day I focused on the vigorous
faith expressed in the Breastplate rather than on my need for
protection. I was not feeling more than ordinarily in need of
protection. When the Breastplate was fictionally placed in an
appropriate place in the life of Patrick, he was thought to have

4. Psalm 21 is another notable example of vigorous faith within the Psalter.

been in danger on a journey that was of crucial importance to his mission. I was not thinking of any crisis ahead in my life when I received the Breastplate as a blessing from God. But I see that in the middle of my journal entries on Wednesday, March 16, the day before St. Patrick's Day, I wrote this prayer: "Lord, I beg you to preserve my sight." (Why I should have felt the need to pray such a prayer I shall explain in the next chapter.)

> I asked to be given—what?
> a word, a way, a direction, a poem—
> that would blossom in my mind.
> Instead I was given a blessing
> and words already given,
> another's words, to be content with,
> words of robust assurance,
> passed across the millennia,
> a torch to carry through the mist.
>
> Unasked I was given an outlook,
> a window to the wide sea,
> to scry at noon and at evening,
> where there are only swirling winds
> a light in the night hours.
> Reading in the late silence,
> eyes failing, from the perils to come
> I invoked protection.

So when I left Alnmouth on Friday to travel to St. Andrews, I took with me three things that I felt God had given me at the friary. First, there was the direction for my life ahead: "keep on keeping on." Second, there was the eighth verse of "St. Patrick's Breastplate," the invocation of Christ's presence with me, a prayer I had memorized. Third, there was the Breastplate hymn itself, with its powerful expression of vigorous faith.

It is important that I recorded all these in my journal. In recent years I have kept a very informal sort of journal only very sporadically. What I wrote on March 16, my second day in Alnmouth, was the first entry since October 21 the previous year. Looking back now at what I wrote on March 16 and 17, I am very glad that I recorded those thoughts (among others). It assures me that I did have them! Otherwise I might have remembered in a way that was too much influenced by what later transpired in this continuing story. I might have exaggerated the way in which these three blessings received in Alnmouth prepared me for what was to come. Reading those journal entries now and reflecting on them, I can only be impressed by God's provision and grateful for the care with which he gave me what I was to need. I did not see that at the time, but I did receive those blessings and wrote about them.

It occurs to me now that this part of the story is rather like a folktale. Before he sets out on an important journey, the hero is given three presents. He sees they are valuable and important. He does not see what roles they are to play during his journey, but, as it turns out, they are exactly what he needs to meet the challenges that confront him. I guess sometimes our lives actually fall into such archetypal narrative patterns. When we live our lives with God, such patterns are ways in which we experience his goodness.

> I bind unto myself today
> The power of God to hold and lead,
> His eye to watch, his might to stay,
> His ear to hearken to my need.

St. Patrick's Breastplate

I bind unto myself today
The strong name of the Trinity,
By invocation of the same,
The Three in One and One in Three.

I bind this day to me for ever,
By power of faith, Christ's Incarnation,
His baptism in Jordan river,
His death on cross for my salvation,
His bursting from the spiced tomb,
His riding up the heavenly way,
His coming at the day of doom,
I bind unto myself today.

I bind unto myself the power
Of the great love of Cherubim,
The sweet "Well done" in judgment hour,
The service of the Seraphim,
Confessors' faith, Apostles' word,
The Patriarchs' prayers, the Prophets' scrolls,
All good deeds done unto the Lord,
And purity of virgin souls.

I bind unto myself today
The virtues of the star-lit heaven,
The glorious sun's life-giving ray,
The whiteness of the moon at even,
The flashing of the lightning free,
The whirling wind's tempestuous shocks,
The stable earth, the deep salt sea
Around the old eternal rocks.

I bind unto myself today
The power of God to hold and lead,
His eye to watch, his might to stay,
His ear to hearken to my need,
The wisdom of my God to teach,
His hand to guide, His shield to ward,
The Word of God to give me speech,
His heavenly host to be my guard.

Against the demon snares of sin,
The vice that gives temptation force,
The natural lusts that war within,
The hostile men that mar my course,
Or few or many, far or nigh,
In every place, and in all hours,
Against their fierce hostility,
I bind to me these holy powers.

Against all Satan's spells and wiles,
Against false words of heresy,
Against the knowledge that defiles,
Against the heart's idolatry,
Against the wizard's evil craft,
Against the death-wound and the burning,
The choking wave, the poisoned shaft,
Protect me, Christ, till Thy returning.

Christ be with me, Christ within me,
Christ behind me, Christ before me,
Christ beside me, Christ to win me,
Christ to comfort and restore me,
Christ beneath me, Christ above me,
Christ in quiet, Christ in danger,
Christ in hearts of all that love me,
Christ in mouth of friend and stranger.

I bind unto myself the Name,
The strong Name of the Trinity,
By invocation of the same,
The Three in One, and One in Three,
Of Whom all nature hath creation,
Eternal Father, Spirit, Word:
Praise to the Lord of my salvation;
Salvation is of Christ the Lord.[1]

---

1. This version was translated from the Old Irish by Mrs. Cecil Frances Alexander in 1889.

6

The Story, Part 2

Losing Sight

I went to physicians to be healed, but the more they treated me
with ointments the more my vision was obscured.

—Tobit 2:10

On September 29, 2015, soon after I turned sixty-nine, my
right eye succumbed to myopic macular degeneration—
suddenly, as it seemed to me. I knew nothing about macular
degeneration. No one had ever told me that people who have
severe short sight, as I do, are at risk of developing, late in
life, a specific form of macular degeneration, called myopic,
that is different from the more common age-related macular
degeneration (AMD) but has much the same effect. On the
evening of September 29, I saw a report on the television news
about a new cure being trialed for AMD. Enough was said
about AMD to make me try covering my left eye to discover

what I could see with my right eye only. I was shocked to find I could no longer read with my right eye. The faint blur I had had at the center of my vision in that eye for some months was now a dark blob through which I could not see and which distorted even the lines of print around it. (The reason I had not noticed this developing loss of sight in my right eye may be that I was unconsciously compensating for it with the use of my left eye.) On the internet I discovered a little about the two sorts of macular degeneration, wet and dry, and that only the former can be treated. I also found the alarming information that if macular degeneration happens to one eye, it is likely to happen to the other. I realized I had to face the possibility of a future, perhaps not distant, in which I would not be able to read. Some of the issues I would have to consider with much more force in 2022 were already on my mind. Looking back a fortnight later, I described them in my journal:

> Would life without reading be endurable? More immediately, what about all my unfinished writing projects? Well—I told myself—my work is for God and it is for God to decide whether he gives me time for it, whether he really wants it—or all of it.

I soon realized I needed to talk to someone about what was happening to my eye. "Thank God for Susan," I wrote in my journal, a thought I had several times again in 2022, as will become clear. Susan is a friend, a former General Practitioner (GP), and like me a member of St. Mark's Church, Newnham.

Before describing Susan's advice, I need to explain why my eye had not been treated in the period when the degeneration was already happening, before I noticed it. In April 2015 I had had an eye examination by an optician, which resulted in my getting reading glasses for the first time (in addition to my distance glasses). The optician, who was young and probably inexperienced, told me that there was degeneration in my right eye and I should get an appointment at the eye clinic at Adden-brooke's Hospital.[1] But she also said there was not much that could be done about it. She may have used the term *macular degeneration*, but she certainly did not explain it. I had no idea it would lead to loss of central vision in the eye. I did not know that it was wet macular degeneration and could be treated if the intervention were made soon enough. I got no sense that there was any urgency about it. Of course, I should have taken more initiative to find out what was really wrong, but I was not used to doing so and had many other things to attend to.

That was in April. When eventually I received notice of an appointment made for me at the eye clinic, it was for July or August (I forget which). But it was the first of three appoint-ments that were subsequently canceled. Then I was given an appointment that I myself had to cancel because I was going to be away. When I asked for a new appointment, it was for March 2016. I was not unduly worried about these delays, though I did think of querying the last one. I guess I naively supposed that if my condition needed urgent treatment, they would not have postponed my appointments so often. I did not reckon with the way such things are handled. I had been fortunate not to have had to attend hospitals very often in my life.

So I was not in any way prepared for the loss of central vision that I was shocked to discover on September 29. The next day I talked with Susan, who advised I get an urgent appointment at the local GP practice. So later that day I saw Dr. C, who thought my story of postponed appointments at Addenbrooke's appall-ing. They should have treated my case as urgent, because wet

1. Addenbrooke's is the principal National Health Service hospital in Cam-bridge. It has a very high reputation.

AMD, which she thought I might have, can be treated so as to prevent further degeneration. She advised I pay for a private consultation at a private hospital in order to get a diagnosis. I have always been opposed to private health care, because it takes resources away from the UK's National Health Service (NHS), but in this case it seemed so important that I get a proper examination of my eye and diagnosis as soon as possible. Susan, also opposed to private health care in principle, also suggested this option to me. Without advice from Susan and Dr. C, it would probably not have occurred to me.

The first appointment I could get was for October 8. Mr. N, who examined me, explained that I had *myopic* macular degeneration, caused by the effect on the eye of a lifetime of severe short sight. This explained why I had macular degeneration at a younger age than is common for age-related macular degeneration, the more common condition. This was comparatively good news, because, with myopic macular degeneration, the chances that the other eye will also develop the condition are much lower than is the case with AMD. (Later, at the Addenbrooke's eye clinic, Mr. O, the consultant, told me the chances of this were very low.) Moreover, a wet form of macular degeneration can be treated. I do not remember whether I thought of paying for private treatment, but I did not in fact choose that option. It was November 12 before I got a consultation with Mr. O at Addenbrooke's and December 18 before I got the first eye injection. I do not know for sure whether in October I still had a chance of benefiting from treatment, other than by preventing further damage. I am inclined to think I did not. The opportunity to rescue my ability to read in that eye was missed earlier, when my appointments were being postponed month by month. But I saw no point in dwelling on what might have been.

Mr. O put me on a course of three injections in the eye, at monthly intervals, which is the standard practice. He said this was in case the injections might help. In fact, they may have stabilized the condition, but no more. I think it must have been from this experience with my right eye that I acquired the conviction that the injections can only stabilize the condition of an eye in which degeneration has begun to occur. They cannot reverse any damage already done. At that stage I didn't really know much about the way they actually work.

Thus I was left with no central vision in one eye. The key features of this are that one cannot see people's faces and cannot read. But I still had one good eye! I still had the sight I needed for all my activities, both eyes supplying peripheral vision, the left eye central vision. For several years this was fine. I did not, of course, ignore the possibility of getting macular degeneration in my left eye, though I did not, as far as I can remember, think that likely. After all, Mr. O had thought it very unlikely. I don't think I took account of the possibility of developing age-related macular degeneration in my left eye. But from time to time I would use the Amsler grid to test my eyes. To use the grid, one focuses one eye on the blob in the center of the grid, in order to see both whether there is any blurred vision in the center and whether one's sight is distorted (when the lines of the grid begin to bend and undulate).

In the two or three years up to 2020, I had been aware of a general decline in the sight in my left eye, which seemed much like my short sight simply getting worse. I began to realize that I needed very good light in order to read. I invested in a Serious Readers light, a standard lamp that enabled me to go on reading in my armchair in my sitting room. The special value of these lamps is that they not only provide a bright light but also replicate, as far as possible, the quality of daylight. My armchair is close to a window, but even so, the daylight was often not sufficient. The Serious Readers lamp made a huge difference. Later I bought two more of them.

A landmark event in my realization of how much my sight was deteriorating was a visit to the Hokusai exhibition at the British Museum in the autumn of 2021. I love the work of this great Japanese artist, and on visits to Japan I had seen many of the hundreds of woodcut prints that he produced over his long and amazingly prolific lifetime. In 2020 the British Museum acquired a very rare artistic treasure: a collection of 103 drawings that Hokusai prepared for a printed book that was to be called *The Great Picture Book of Everything*. The book was never produced, and so these drawings are unique. In other cases Hokusai's drawings were used to make woodcuts, and so the drawings themselves did not survive. These drawings are therefore exceptional. Each is almost exactly the size of a modern postcard.

Naturally, I looked forward to seeing them, but it did not take me long to realize that I could not. They were exhibited behind glass at a reasonably short distance, but even when I was able to put my face right up to the glass, I was unable to see them. I could see the rectangular shapes, of course, but I could not make out anything of the delicate drawings within them. I had become used to finding it difficult to read captions describing the contents of exhibitions, often because it was hard to get close enough to these labels, but I had never before found it impossible to see the exhibits themselves. It was some consolation to see the reproductions of the drawings in the book of the exhibition. These are larger than the originals and easier to see and appreciate than the originals would have been even with good eyesight. Moreover, as a friend of the museum, I got free entry to the exhibition and so had not wasted money. But all the same, I was severely shocked to discover the limits to which my eyesight was now reduced. There would now be cultural experiences unavailable to me, though perhaps not many. But I did not yet envisage the possibility of not being able to read books.

So far this chapter has told the backstory to the main narrative. I can now pick up the main story by returning to the three days I spent at the Franciscan friary in Alnmouth in March 2022. Each morning I bought a daily newspaper, mainly because the Russian invasion of Ukraine had occurred very recently and I wanted to keep abreast of the news. I also took several books to read. In the big bay window of my room, I was able to read in excellent daylight, but I was conscious of needing to sit where that light fell on the page. There was a very bright desk light in the room, but it was not a Serious Readers light. Used to depending on my Serious Readers lamp at home, I was conscious of the difference. I did a lot of reading in the evening, because after supper there was little else to do. I knew I was struggling a bit to read. Hence the prayer I wrote in my journal at that time: "Lord, I beg you to preserve my sight." I would not commonly have said "beg" in a prayer.

From Alnmouth I took the train to St. Andrews, where I had planned to stay a few days in my holiday home. For the first couple of days, I did not feel entirely well: "A dull general headache that aspirin would not shift and a more specific headache on one side of my forehead." I did not record and cannot remember on which side of my forehead it was. If I knew it was the left side, I would now be able to connect it more assuredly with what was happening to my left eye. Initially I thought I might be coming down with Covid again. I knew that having had it in January did not make me immune from getting it a second time. At this time, one in fourteen people in Scotland and one in twenty people in England had Covid—the highest figures since the start of the pandemic (though hospitalizations were much lower than during the height of the pandemic). But I tested negative. I became convinced the headache resulted from straining my eyes reading in Alnmouth.

Over the next few days I enjoyed meeting some friends and former colleagues. But on Wednesday afternoon I looked at the Amsler grid and saw with alarm that my eyesight had suddenly got worse. This was the first time I saw horizontal lines as wavy lines, a distortion of my vision that has remained until now and is going to remain. As a result of my experience with my right eye in the past, I was acutely conscious of the need to get an injection in the eye as soon as possible, if this serious deterioration was to be stopped. I decided I needed to travel to Cambridge the next day on the earliest possible train. I made an appointment to see a doctor at my GP practice in Cambridge in the late afternoon. I also phoned the Spire Hospital to inquire about an appointment with Mr. N, the ophthalmologist who had diagnosed the macular degeneration in my right eye, but found that I would have to wait until well into the next week. It seemed best to stick with the NHS.

I got to Cambridge just in time for the appointment with Dr. Z, a GP I had not previously met. I was very disappointed that she failed to grasp the urgency of the situation and told me that I had to see an optician before I could get an appointment at the eye clinic. She advised me not to go to A&E (the Accident and Emergency clinic at Addenbrooke's). I simply insisted that I knew my eye would continue to suffer irreversible damage unless something were done very soon. I must have prevailed much as the widow prevailed on the unjust judge in Jesus's parable. Dr. Z said that, just because I was so insistent, she would do something she was not supposed to do. She would ask the AMD clinic for an appointment for me. I did not know how long I would have to wait for that.

When I got home, I opened my email. I became even more alarmed because the wavy lines were so prominent, so *wavy*.

The distortion was more evident than on the Amsler grid. I decided to go to A&E. To my relief, when I explained my problem to the nurse who was triaging the people in the queue waiting to get into A&E, she sent me straight to the Urgent Treatment Centre, which is staffed by GPs. The doctor I saw was understanding and recognized the urgency. He made an appointment for me to have an urgent scan at the eye clinic and to see a registrar the following day (Friday). I admit I did not then know what a registrar (in a hospital context) is and only later discovered that a registrar is a doctor in the last phase of training, after being a junior doctor. No doubt this reveals how little experience of hospitals I have had, though perhaps also that I never watch hospital soaps or reality programs on TV.

My appointment for the scan was at 2:30, and it must have been about 2:40 when the scan was actually done (the time will prove to be significant in the next chapter). But then I had to wait about four hours to see the doctor (Dr. R). When I did eventually see him, he explained that there were seven doctors in ophthalmology off with Covid. Those who were there were plainly rushed off their feet. No doubt there were also nurses off for the same reason. The wait was the more difficult because none of those waiting had any idea how long the wait might be or what place in the queue they occupied. The drinks machine was not working, and I dared not go elsewhere to find a coffee, for fear of missing my turn. I had nothing to read (I had not brought anything because I knew the light would not be good enough). I remember that I prayed the "Christ be with me" prayer that I had committed to memory in Alnmouth. I guess I prayed in other ways too. I was in a state of considerable anxiety, which made the waiting worse. I am sure it was the same for some of the others who were also waiting. Those of us still waiting in the late afternoon realized things were generally shutting down and wondered if we would be seen at all. I know there was nothing exceptional about this experience. People wait in A&E for much longer times.

Eventually, a nurse brought some cups of tea, but by then I was with Dr. R, who saw me in two stages because he didn't know enough about macular degeneration and wanted to consult his colleagues. I realized later that he did not know that myopic macular degeneration is a wet rather than a dry form of the condition (he was puzzled that I had had injections in the right eye). But he told me the relevant feature of the scan: a new and abnormal blood vessel (called choroidal neovascularization) had developed behind the macula. This was apparently the cause of the distortion of my vision. He said there was no immediate danger of things getting worse. On the computer he found I had an appointment in the AMD clinic on April 4 (in ten days' time). (This was the appointment Dr. Z had asked for.) He asked them, should they have an earlier slot, to bring that appointment forward. If anything changed, I could phone the emergency eye clinic and get another appointment there. He was doing his best, and I had more peace of mind after talking with him. What kept my anxiety level high, however, was that I knew the appointment on April 4 (or earlier) would not be the occasion for an injection. It would be for assessing my need for an injection, and then, presumably, I would have to join a queue.

What I was facing, at that time and for weeks to come, was the possibility of losing altogether my ability to read. Since that was what had happened in my right eye, I had every reason to think that, without quick and effective medical intervention, it would happen in my left eye as well. Sometimes I supposed I might without further warning suddenly find a large blob in the center of my vision in my left eye, as I had done in my right eye. Might I just wake up one morning, open my eyes, put on my glasses, and find exactly that? The damage would be done, and no injection could then reverse it. That seemed a real—and terrifying—possibility.

I even tried to imagine what I would immediately do if that happened. Unable to see the keys on the phone or to use email, how would I even tell anyone what had happened? None of the ways people with that condition have for coping with it was in place in my home or my life. If I didn't think too much about that possibility, I guess it always lurked somewhere in my consciousness.

On March 28, I wrote in my journal,

One thing seems certain: eventually I will lose central vision in my left eye. I just hope I get time to prepare properly for that. Lord, have mercy.

Of course, losing my ability to read would be massively life-changing for me, far more so than for many people. It would go far beyond the difficulties of navigating daily life, because reading books has always been such a huge part of my life.

7

A Message from Taiwan

REM sleep can therefore be considered as a state characterized by strong activation in visual, motor, emotional and autobiographical memory regions of the brain, yet a relative deactivation in regions that control rational thought.

—Matthew Walker, *Why We Sleep*

At 2:41 p.m. on Friday, March 25, an email arrived in my inbox. I was at the eye clinic at Addenbrooke's Hospital at the time and did not see it until I arrived home in the evening. The email had come to me via my website. I am used to getting emails by that means from people I do not know. So I was not surprised that I did not recognize the name: Li, HsiuYu. (Li is her family name, which in Chinese names precedes the personal name.) It turned out, however, to be the name of someone I had met in 2017 but had not been in contact with since then. I will quote part of the email:

This is a message from Taiwan and I am the person who told you about a dream about a Taiwanese Professor who also studied under Prof. Moltmann on the Saturday night when you stayed overnight at an elder's house. That night when you walked into the church I was conducting the church choir. Anyway, I am writing this message because few days ago the word "Cambridge" appeared in my dream, and I do not know why. My only connection with "Cambridge" is to know you are living at Cambridge and a young missionary who was from Cambridge, but died in Taiwan in 1993, Jonathan Sturtridge. . . . So, I checked the website you gave to me and write this message to you. . . . Since I dreamed about you I remember you in my prayer and may God protect you in this worldly pandemic time.

Pastor Li (as I remembered her) is a pastor in the Presbyterian Church of Taiwan. I met her in 2017 when I went to Taiwan to give the keynote lectures at a conference on the care of creation for Christian leaders and Christians involved in ecological projects in East Asia. Before the conference, the Taiwanese Christian organization that was hosting it had arranged for me to preach and lecture at a church in Koupi, in the southwest of Taiwan, in the area of one of the indigenous people of the island, the Siraya. The church was without a pastor at the time, and so I was hosted by one of the elders, Mr. Hsiau. I stayed Saturday night at his home, a big house surrounded by thick forest. At breakfast on Sunday I met Pastor Li, who (as she says in her email) was there to conduct the church choir at the morning service. I don't recall what we talked about at breakfast, but I met her again later in Taipei. She associated me with Jürgen Moltmann because, although I did not in fact study with him, I had written books about his theology.

I found the conference a hugely encouraging event and learned a lot from other speakers, especially those involved in practical local projects. They seemed to find the theological approaches to ecological matters that I was providing really helpful for their work. After the conference I was scheduled to make a visit to a church in Haulien on the east coast of Taiwan, again to preach and lecture on ecological themes. But Typhoon Nesat was approaching from the east, and it was thought inadvisable for me to make the trip. So I remained in Taipei for three nights before flying on to Japan. I stayed in the YMCA Hotel, which I expected to be rather basic accommodation. In fact, I had a very comfortable and well-equipped room. I was able to rest and also to do some sightseeing in and around the city. I still wear the baseball cap emblazoned with a Chinese dragon that I bought in Taipei.

The typhoon caused a lot of flooding in parts of Taiwan. Thousands of people had to be evacuated from their homes, but none died and only a few were injured. In Taipei there were very high winds and heavy rain. From my hotel window I watched some people clinging to railings and lampposts as they made their way to shelter. But the following morning all was quiet, and when I took a walk, I could see very little damage. What there was had no doubt been efficiently cleared away by a populace very used to such wild weather. It was the closest I have come to a typhoon. But the experience brought home to me how very vulnerable Taiwan and other places on the eastern rim of Asia are, increasingly so as extreme weather becomes more frequent. The typhoon that hit Japan a few weeks earlier was more destructive than this one.

Pastor Li wanted to talk with me, and on Sunday afternoon we went to Starbucks, where I had a coffee but she did not. (During this visit to Taiwan I discovered that most Chinese people do not drink coffee much and find it odd that Western people need several cups of it to get through the day.) This conversation, rather than the one we had in Koupi, was the one I remembered, whereas she remembered the latter. That's how memories work.

I seem to remember that we stayed at Starbucks until it closed and continued talking in the hotel lobby. By her own admission, Pastor Li is a talkative person. She is also highly intelligent. She has a PhD from the University of Edinburgh and other degrees from the Pacific School of Theology, Princeton Theological Seminary, and Fuller Theological Seminary in the United States. For several years she worked in China, teaching in the churches in an undercover manner. (She had to terminate this ministry in 2019, as Covid began to spread through China.)

Pastor Li believes she has a spiritual gift of dreams and dream interpretation. She receives messages from God in dreams, which are typically meant for other people, to whom she communicates them once she has divined their meaning. I cannot recall the dreams she told me about when we met in Taipei. I recall not being very convinced that they were genuinely messages from God, but I consciously withheld judgment. I was not in a position to tell.

I will give one example, of which she told me quite recently. (She may have told me about it in Taipei, but I can't remember.) I choose it partly because it concerns someone I knew: John O'Neill, who was professor of New Testament at New College, Edinburgh, and who died in 2003. When Pastor Li was working for her PhD at New College, John was living in retirement in Edinburgh. She met him because they went to the same church. Here is a slightly edited version of her own account:

> I dreamt that Prof. O'Neill was limping and leaned over to hold the back of a chair. On Sunday I tried to find him to tell him the dream, but he was not at church. The following Sunday I saw him and told him the dream. He said that the previous Sunday he had been in hospital.
>
> Then I heard that Prof. O'Neill was hospitalized again. I went to the hospital to visit him and afterward I had the second dream.

I saw a woman sitting on a bed knitting. Even though I did not know what disease he had, I guessed the dream was telling me that Prof. O'Neill was "knitting a dream that he can get well." But on my second visit, I dared not tell him this, even though he told me, "Your dream is real." I only told him I had had a dream gift since I was at Fuller Seminary in USA. In my third dream, a hospital-type bed was upended against the wall. Someone took us to the counter to check out. I knew the dream was telling me that Prof. O'Neill was "checking out"—not in a good sense but checking out from the world. Again, I dared not tell him the dream.

Not long after that dream, I heard that Prof. O'Neill had passed away. He did check out from the hospital, but so that he would be able to end his life at home. After the funeral, I sent an email about the three dreams to his family and let them know that it was God's timing to take him away, for God had showed me beforehand through the dreams. I still pray for his three daughters to experience God's blessing.

I have to admit I tend to be somewhat skeptical about messages in dreams or about any claims (such as those of Sigmund Freud and psychoanalysts of his persuasion) to find significance in dreams. As far as I understand it, the science now tells us that dreams are produced by the brain's activity of organizing our memories while we sleep, selecting from the memories of the day which to store permanently and where to file them in the brain's extremely complex filing system. This is why, when we remember dreams, they frequently relate—though often in bizarre ways—to events and thoughts of the preceding day. The fact that our memory of dreams is usually very fleeting, quickly lost after we wake, is surely related to the lack of meaning for us. If we remembered much of the hours of dreams we have every night, our minds would be encumbered with a lot of useless and meaningless junk. The practice of keeping dream notebooks to record dreams before they are forgotten seems to me pointless. Most of what we dream is a mere by-product of the important work the brain can do only when we are asleep and is of no significance in itself.

I rarely remember much from dreams. Those that do stick in my mind at least a little while after waking often seem to be dreams that have affected me emotionally for some reason. A few fragments of dreams I remember because I woke from them with a feeling of deep happiness. Sometimes I wake from bad dreams, but I rarely have nightmares and certainly not the recurring nightmares that afflict some people. I can't recall that I have ever dreamed about God or angels or heaven. Since God is so often in my waking consciousness, it seems odd that he never seems to be in my dreams. I cannot explain that. I remember a dream in which a friend I knew to be a strong believer revealed that he didn't actually believe anything at all. That was a horribly disturbing dream, even though I didn't for a moment, once awake, think it was true. Of course, some dreams are memorable because they are so absurd. I once dreamed that a group of people was having a picnic on top of the West Gate in St. Andrews. The fact that I told one or two people about that dream may be a reason I have remembered it. My brain filed my remembering it somewhere.

Sometimes dreams seem to pick up elements of dreams I have had in previous nights. There are several houses that I own only in dreams and seem to visit or think about in successive dreams on numerous nights. They are connected with geographical locations that are partly reminiscent of places I know but partly extend those locations in fictional ways that again sometimes perdure from dream to dream. I do not know why this happens, but I have yet to find any significance in it. People in my dreams, on the other hand, seem not to have this characteristic. People I know appear in my dreams frequently but entirely randomly as far as I have noticed. I remember them from real life, not from previous dreams, and that, I think, is a good thing. But I must stress that I have not attempted to study my dreams. I remember mere fragments of them and rarely take much notice of them.

Extremely rarely I have had a vivid dream that stuck with me and later seemed prophetic. I once had a dream in which, near the house or flat where I lived, there was a gate into a park. At the time there was no gate into a park anywhere I was familiar with. But for some reason the phrase "the gate into the park" stuck in my mind. It was somehow connected with attractive prospects beyond the gate. Other features of that dream I also remembered but have since largely forgotten. But many years later I found myself living not far from a gate into a park. I was scarcely aware of it when I bought the house, but sometime later I realized I had found "the gate into the park." The park into which it led was unremarkable. I rarely visited it for its own sake. But across the park was the way to the countryside. Almost immediately beyond the park were fields and woods. I walked that way habitually. It was, as I think back on it, a hugely important aspect of my environment at that time. (There was another route to the countryside that I also took, but less often.) "The gate into the park," with its connotations of attractions beyond it, seemed to deserve its status as a fragment I remembered from a dream. When such things happen, they naturally seem significant, perhaps more to me than to some more pragmatic people. But I readily concede that the link I saw between the dream and the much later reality could easily be purely coincidental.

I certainly do not wish to deny that God may speak to people in dreams.[1] Occasionally, it happens in Scripture. In the prophetic

1. G. Scott Sparrow, *I Am with You Always: True Stories of Encounters with Jesus* (London: BCA [Macmillan], 1995), collects many reports of dreams in which Jesus appears and speaks to the person dreaming. Most of them seem

literature of the Hebrew Bible there seems to be no clear distinction between dreams and visions. Daniel had revelatory visions while dreaming in the nighttime (Dan. 7:1–2). In some cases God speaks quite clearly in dreams, as he did to Solomon (1 Kings 3:5–15), but often dreams are obscure until interpreted, like those that Joseph was fortunately able to explain (Gen. 40:1–41:36).

In the book of Job, Elihu, the youngest of the comforters, who speaks last, is determined to break down what he considers Job's arrogance and to coax Job into admitting the sins he is sure Job must have committed. This is one attempt:

> God speaks first in one way,
> and then in another, although we do not realize it.
> In dreams and in night visions,
> when slumber has settled on humanity and people are
>   asleep in bed,
> he speaks in someone's ear,
> frightens a person with apparitions
> to turn that person away from some action
> and to curb pride.
> And thus he preserves the soul from the abyss,
> that life from passing down the Canal. (Job 33:14–18
>   RNJB)

We must assume this missed its mark because Job had no such nightmares. The idea that nightmares may terrify sinners into repenting is an unusual one, but it may be what the rich man in Jesus's parable had in mind when he asked for Lazarus to warn his brothers of the postmortem fate that awaited them unless they repented (Luke 16:27–31).

---

to me easily explicable as quite ordinary dreams rather than divinely given ones. Jesus says just the sorts of things people might expect him to say, often in familiar scriptural language.

One of the most significant dreams in the New Testament is the vision that persuaded Paul to revise his mission plans and cross from Asia into Europe. Luke calls it a "vision" that Paul had "during the night" (Acts 16:9). Probably, like Daniel's night visions, it happened in a dream. Paul saw "a man of Macedonia pleading with him and saying, 'Come over to Macedonia and help us'" (16:9). I guess most readers assume that this is all that Paul saw and that its message was clear. It must have been clear enough to convince Paul that this was the direction God now wished his missionary travels to go. But if this "vision" occurred in a dream, it can only have been one brief episode in the usual very rapid succession of weirdly connected events and changes of scenes that are the substance of all dreams. Presumably what happened was that this episode survived the process of forgetting most of a dream that occurs on waking. It seemed to be important and to mean something. Since he was in Troas and some other directions of travel had already been barred to him by divine guidance, the idea of taking ship to Macedonia must have occurred to him already as at least one possibility. The dream was picking up, as dreams do, something that had been in his mind the preceding day. But it came to him with the authority of a divinely given message. So perhaps this is how a message from God can be received in a dream. Just as "the gate into the park," for reasons I cannot comprehend, emerged from a dream of mine as a powerful image in my memory, so, I imagine, the man pleading with Paul to come over and help the people in Macedonia stuck vividly in his mind. He had been seeking God's will for the future direction of his ministry, had perhaps already wondered whether this was it, and the vision spoke directly to his need for guidance. Since Paul was a man who lived closely with God and sincerely sought to go where God directed him, we should assume that this vision was truly a message from God.

I have never knowingly received a message from God in a dream. When fragments from dreams have stuck in my memory, it has never occurred to me to understand them as messages from God. In retrospect I cannot think of any that would make sense as such a message, but perhaps I might have thought otherwise had I been expecting such a means of communication to be used by God. This lengthy reflection on dreams is designed to explain why, in late March 2022, I was not likely to be easily convinced that God was saying something to me in a very obscure way through someone else's dream.

In Pastor Li's dream, the word *Cambridge*, repeated, apparently came out of the blue. (She seems to have seen it, not heard it.) She was not aware of any reason why it would have occurred to her. Of course, the complexities of the brain's filing system are such that this doesn't necessarily require any special explanation. What impressed me about her communication was the timing. Her email reached my inbox at 2:41, which must be exactly or nearly exactly when I was getting my eye scanned at the eye clinic for the first time. The dream itself occurred "a few days ago"—which was when I was becoming aware of this serious problem in the eyesight of my left eye. If I am somewhat skeptical about messages in dreams, I believe strongly that God is often at work in "coincidences." So in my reply to Pastor Li the following day, I wrote:

> It is really remarkable that you must have seen "Cambridge" in your dream just when I was getting concerned about what was happening to my vision (Wednesday). It seems to me that God's purpose in this must be to send me an assurance of his love and concern for me at this time. It is a great blessing.

When I later thought about why God should have chosen this apparently odd way to give me such an assurance, it occurred to me that for *me* to be convinced of the reality of such a message, it needed to come from an unlikely source (someone who knew nothing about my particular need at that time) and, by a striking coincidence, at the right time. If a friend who knew all about the situation had received a message assuring me of God's love and concern, I might not have taken it seriously as a specific communication from God. It was what such a person would readily suppose God would say to me at such a time. Pastor Li's dream was something I had to take seriously. I think it is important that she did not attempt to interpret the dream herself. She did not know it was for me before she contacted me to find out if it was, and she did not tell me what she thought it meant. It proved relevant to me in a way she did not know.

Looking back now, I see no reason to take it less seriously than my conviction that God had given the three blessings I received in Alnmouth. Through a surprising means, a very obscure dream in Taiwan, God was continuing to provide for me what I would need to get me through this crisis. The value this message had for me can be seen in this reflection that I wrote in my journal on March 28:

> God has got me through some very difficult times in my life. He will get me through this—and the message from Taiwan was a wonderful assurance of that. He will be with me whatever. In his strength I can have vigorous faith (as in St. Patrick's Breastplate).

Subsequently, Pastor Li told me of additional dreams that she thought applied to me, but I was not convinced. They were dreams in which professors better known to her appeared, and she took these figures to be symbols standing in for me. That seemed an arbitrary way of interpreting the dreams. (On the other hand, she says, "To understand the possible meaning of dreams takes gifts, training in literature and language, professional knowledge in dreams and experience in dreaming." So perhaps I should be more cautious about rejecting her interpretations. But I cannot help forming an opinion on whether a dream refers to me.) But my doubts about these later dreams do not seem to be a reason for doubting the relevance of the "Cambridge" dream that spoke to me a message of God's concern for me at the right time.

8

The Story, Part 3

"God Will Be with Me Whatever"

When you pass through the waters, I will be with you;
and through the rivers, they shall not overwhelm you.

—Isaiah 43:2

God will be with me whatever": I wrote these words in
my journal on March 28, when I was confronting the
possibility—which truly scared me—of losing my ability to
read. It was during a week of high anxiety about whether I
would get treatment for my eye in time to prevent further deterioration. A week later I wrote that this "feels like the most difficult time of my whole life," but I also repeated my affirmation
of "vigorous faith," this time addressed to God: "I will always
know you with me." The combination of anxiety and trust in
God might seem paradoxical—should not vigorous faith banish
anxiety?—but it seems to me entirely natural. It is often in such

times of anxiety and stress that God can seem very near. It is in our weakness that we know the strength he gives (a theme to which I shall return). When we brave difficult times without anxiety, we can too easily assume it is in our own strength rather than placing our confidence in God.

Though I doubt that I consciously recalled this at the time, I had in fact reflected on the theme of God's presence "with" people in the Bible in my most recently published book.[1] I began with Jacob's dream at Bethel, in which God promises, "Know that I am with you and will keep you wherever you go" (Gen. 28:15). The motif of God's unfailing and protective presence "with" Jacob recurs throughout the story of his life (31:3; 35:3; 46:4). At the end of his very long life, he sums it up: "the God who has been my shepherd all my life to this day" (48:15). This image of the shepherd who accompanies the sheep harks back to Jacob's employment as a shepherd, looking after the flocks of his father-in-law (30:29–43). Jacob knew well what it meant to be a shepherd. The shepherd must lead the flock to pasture and water, but most basically he must be with the sheep at all times. He must be there with them in order to protect and care for them.

The same image is developed in the well-known Psalm 23, which I believe in my day we all learned by heart at school. At the heart of the psalm—literally its central words—is the affirmation "for you are with me" (Ps. 23:4). In a life with God, his guidance, provision, and protection are important, as Jacob and the psalmist knew well, but in all such experiences the center and source is God's presence "with us." We could see the psalm as making Jacob's experience available to all who read it and who let it feed a vigorous faith in God. This must

1. Richard Bauckham, *Who Is God? Key Moments of Biblical Revelation* (Grand Rapids: Baker Academic, 2020), 5–12.

be the reason why it has long been the most popular of all
the psalms. Discovering God's presence "with" us in our lives
may be the most important discovery anyone can make, for,
once made, it colors all the experiences of a life, including the
most difficult. Psalm 23 has come into its own in many people's
lives, especially when they have faced dangers, suffering, and
death. The traditional translation of verse 4 (which may not be
the most accurate) speaks of going "through the valley of the
shadow of death" (KJV), and this has made the verse a source
of faith and courage for people approaching death. But it can be
translated "through the darkest valley" (NRSV). In this more
general sense, it could certainly apply to the very dark valley—
what felt like the most difficult time of my life—through which
I was traveling in this stretch of my lifelong journey with God.

Psalm 23 surely fed into the composition of "St. Patrick's
Breastplate," especially the verse I had made my own: "Christ
be with me . . . Christ to comfort and restore me." But "comfort
and restore" is not a literal translation of the Old Irish, and so
at this point it would seem to be the translator, Mrs. Alexander, who had in mind the words of Psalm 23 in the King James
Version ("thy rod and thy staff they comfort me" [v. 4]; "he
restoreth my soul" [v. 3]). The Breastplate does not use the
image of shepherding, but the emphasis on Christ "with" me,
spelled out in all dimensions, corresponds to the heart of the
psalm. In a more literal version than the most familiar version,
the Breastplate reads:

> Christ with me,
> Christ before me,
> Christ behind me,
> Christ in me,
> Christ beneath me,
> Christ above me,

> Christ on my right,
> Christ on my left,
> Christ when I lie down,
> Christ when I sit down,
> Christ when I arise.

Much of the Breastplate, as an invocation of God's protection from all evil forces on a perilous journey, gives extended expression to the thought of the psalm in verse 4:

> Even though I walk through the darkest valley,
>   I fear no evil;
> for you are with me.

The psalm refers to the God of Israel, the Breastplate to Christ, reminding us that in the New Testament God's presence "with" people takes the form of the presence of Jesus Christ. He himself is Immanuel, which means "God with us" (Isa. 7:14; Matt. 1:23), and at the end of Matthew's Gospel he promises, "I am with you always, to the end of the age" (Matt. 28:20).

Though I am sure that this scriptural background had formed my thoughts about and attitudes toward the presence of God in my life, my own affirmation was no mere quotation. I phrased it spontaneously with reference to my real situation: "God will be with me whatever." However things turned out, even if I did lose the ability to read altogether, I knew that God would be with me, making a difference. I was not confident that he would necessarily protect me from such an outcome, much as I fervently hoped that he would, but I knew that whatever happened would be his loving will for me and that he would protect me, giving me the courage and strength to go through that darkest valley, leading me through, caring for me on that journey. I never lost that assurance of his presence with me.

The ten days following my first visit to the eye clinic were hugely stressful. I hoped that the appointment I had for April 4 might be brought forward, as Dr. R had requested. Not only was it not brought forward; it was actually canceled! However, I soon discovered that my case was thought to merit an appointment with a consultant ophthalmologist, Mr. K. This was arranged for April 5. All the time I was conscious of the urgency with which I needed to get an injection in the eye before further degeneration occurred. At first I thought the condition of my eye was stable, but by Saturday, April 2, it seemed to me that it was worsening. The wavy lines were getting more wavy, I thought, and I was finding reading difficult for that reason. A feature of that distortion that has remained is that when I hold something close to my eyes, the lines are not distorted but straight. But that meant, at that time, that I could read only by holding a book close to my eyes or getting close to a computer screen. I feared, of course, that the situation was going to be permanent and that my sight would continue to get worse until I got an injection. By the time I got an injection, would I have any reading ability left?

It was in the midst of such anxiety that I wrote in my journal a sentence that I have seen in retrospect as hugely important:

Whatever happens, God will be leading me deeper into his love and further along the way of Jesus Christ.

This affirmation of vigorous faith in God's loving care and purpose for me was what carried me through that difficult period. But it did not dispel the anxiety. I went on to write:

I am so worried. I fear that I shall never again be able to enjoy reading a book, even if I can just manage to read slowly. It will

*be just an effort. The enjoyment of reading a book has been
an almost daily experience since childhood. Nothing at all can
take the place of that. This is a very hard test, Lord, very hard.*

The previous week, when I went into the center of Cambridge to shop, as I usually do once a week, I went to Heffers bookshop to browse. It had long been my habit, on nearly every shopping trip into Cambridge, to visit one of the bookshops: Heffers or Waterstones or, less often, the Cambridge University Press shop. Just browsing the new books is a great pleasure. Indeed, I often reflected that one of the advantages of Cambridge over most other cities is that it has such excellent bookshops. But now I reflected that visiting bookshops would no longer be a pleasure if all I could do would be to look at the covers of books I could not possibly ever read. I would feel like an alcoholic in a very good wine shop.

While I didn't actually move to Cambridge for the sake of the bookshops, an important factor in my decision to retire to Cambridge was the libraries. For my academic interests, I doubt there is anywhere with better libraries: the University Library (a copyright library that receives copies of all books published in the UK), Tyndale House (a very fine specialist library for biblical studies), the Divinity Faculty Library, and other specialist libraries that I sometimes use (such as the Classics Library and the Middle Eastern Studies Library). All such resources would be of little or no use to me if reading became really difficult.

I thought such thoughts the day before my appointment to see Mr. K. I spell them out here to illustrate why the prospect of losing central vision in both eyes so appalled me. Such a prospect affects different people very differently. I can now compare myself with someone whose reflections I read online recently. At the age of fifty-four, two decades younger than me, a woman was diagnosed with a rare form of macular degeneration that, like mine, is due to having severe short sight. It is different from the form I have but similar in its effects. At first she refused to admit even to herself that her life would really be affected, because she did not want her life to change. The changes that she refers to and that inevitably did happen were that she could no longer drive and could not stay in her job as a nurse. A normally sociable person, she suddenly felt she would be stuck in the family home forever.

Of course, it is not difficult to see how these effects could be devastating, especially for someone of her age. She is not ready for even the somewhat more restricted life that many people ease comfortably into in their seventies. But as I compared my case to hers, it struck me that she said nothing about reading. I do not drive a car. My work (no longer paid employment but hugely important to me) is mostly done in my study at home, except for visits to libraries within easy walking distance. My social life largely focuses on church (a ten minutes' walk from home) and friends who live within walking distance. I am used to getting buses and taxis when I do need to travel further within the Cambridge area, or trains to go elsewhere. But for me, not being able to read would be massively life-changing.

My point is that there can be no neutral measurement of how bad losing central vision is for anyone. It may be very bad for someone in one way, for another in another way. For some people, it may not be quite as bad as for others. I am sure some people reacted to my news (in which the only effect I spoke about was not being able to read or only with difficulty) by thinking that surely that would not be as devastating as I thought. After all, there are audiobooks, some people pointed out, and the radio and podcasts. You can even get computers to read stuff to you. But, in fact, just as the woman I have been quoting felt that the whole world outside her home was suddenly closed to her, so I felt that a whole world in which I had lived, and also worked, for so much of my life seemed to be closing to me. That was the world of books. With people who tell me that this would be devastating in the same way for them, I feel a special kinship.

The waiting room in the eye clinic was still configured according to the social distancing requirements of the pandemic. The chairs were placed where marks on the floor indicated, each distanced from others beside, behind, and in front of it. This layout seemed to emphasize the essential isolation of each patient in their private anxieties and fears. Very little was said, even by those who arrived with a companion. Hardly anyone was reading. No one brought coffee or tea in with them. I imagined that some of them, habituated to this situation, were stolidly resigned to waiting, while others were on edge, coming to attention every time a name was called, worried what their diagnosis might be. The arrangement of the chairs reduced somewhat the capacity of the room, so that sometimes people had to sit in the corridor, waiting for a vacant chair in the room.

By preference I sat near the back of the room, from where I could see all the doors from which doctors emerged from time to time to summon a patient by name. Nurses and doctors called all patients by their first name, and for the most part, nurses and doctors themselves were known by their first name. Rare exceptions seemed to be the most senior consultants, such as Mr. O and Mr. N. At the time I did not actually know the surname of the consultant I was waiting to see, although I am calling him Mr. K here.

While waiting I prayed earnestly that he would recognize the urgency of my need, and it was a great relief that he did. I told him briefly that books were hugely important to my life and my work and that I was terrified of losing the ability to read. To my surprise and relief, he arranged for me to have the first of the course of eye injections there and then, in effect jumping the queue. (Since the procedure is quick, I doubt anyone else was disadvantaged by this.) Preparing for the eye injection involves having drops placed in the eye to anesthetize it. In this instance, the drops were not effective enough, for I felt a sharp stab of pain when the needle went in. The pain made me move slightly, and so the doctor performing the operation felt the need to check with Mr. K to ensure that nothing had gone wrong. It had not. I was free to get the bus home. I remembered that six years earlier, when I had injections in my right eye, I was asked to wait fifteen minutes and served tea and biscuits. No longer. The service was provided by volunteers, and volunteers were not allowed in the hospital during the pandemic.

These minor drawbacks notwithstanding, I was elated. I had not expected to get the injection so soon. I felt I was now safe from further deterioration of my sight.

From the time of my first visit to the eye clinic, I wanted people to know what was happening, and I knew that I needed prayer. Since the beginning of the pandemic, my family (my sister and brother-in-law and their children and grandchildren) had had a regular Zoom meeting every Saturday evening. I knew it would not be easy to broach this subject and explain it in the context of the meeting itself, and so I wrote them an email in advance of the meeting.

I also emailed the members of the church home group I belonged to and asked for their prayers. This was then a group of fifteen people (including me). About half of them had been meeting throughout the pandemic every Tuesday evening on Zoom. (Some joined the group during that period, and two others left the UK in 2021.) I think all of us would say that the group was a lifeline in the various circumstances of the lockdowns and restrictions, when meaningful contact in person was rarely possible. We continued our regular practice of group Bible study throughout. We also shared news and concerns. It became a support group in difficult times. It was very rare for any of us to miss a meeting. (In those times it was rare to have a clash of commitments.) In this way the pandemic had given me a circle of Christian friends to whom I naturally turned for prayer and moral support in this difficult time of my life. I knew they would offer (as they did) practical support if I needed it. Having lived alone for most of my adult life, I have learned to rely on my own resources for most purposes and have become, both emotionally and practically, a very independent person. While I have never lacked good friends, I have tried not to expect too much from them. People's lives are such that for very good reason they are not necessarily available when you might need them. When I moved to Newnham, I initially knew no one in the neighborhood. I got to know some people at St. Mark's quite well, but it was the pandemic that turned this group of six or seven people into friends I could confidently expect to support me. The pandemic was tragic for those who lost loved ones, a cause of considerable hardship for many, but my experience is far from the only example of the way many people also found it an occasion for receiving generous gifts from God.

Later I shared my news with a wider circle of friends in Cambridge, elsewhere in the UK, and overseas. Many sent messages and promised to pray. Throughout the difficult weeks to come, I felt accompanied by prayer. At one point I recalled the story of the paralyzed man whose friends got him into the presence of Jesus by tearing up part of the roof and lowering him into the house. It is a parable of our need for others to pray for us. People who are sick often find it difficult to pray themselves. I was not, in that respect, like the paralyzed man. I had no difficulty getting into the presence of Jesus and putting my needs to him myself. But in such a situation, it is not good to be independent of others unless (as can happen) we have no choice. Part of the way that God works among us is through the sharing of needs in prayer and the sharing of thanksgiving and joy for answered prayer. In that way our lives are open in love at once toward each other and toward God. When we pray for each other, God's love embraces us all.

I have explained how the possibility of losing my ability to read felt so severe a threat simply because reading had always been so huge a feature of my life. But there was another aspect: it was a kind of challenge to my vocation. Had I been wrong to discern in Alnmouth that my calling now was to "keep on keeping on"? I think that when we are on a path of devotion to God and seriously seek his direction at key points in our lives, we may expect to receive it. But such discernments of God's will are far from infallible. I could have been wrong in this instance, but I was not about to conclude that. One obstacle to doing so concerned the stage I had reached in the specific project of academic research and writing in which I had been engaged throughout the pandemic.

I had come to call it my "pandemic project" because I began it around the time the pandemic began and it became the project on which I mainly worked throughout the pandemic. But there was also a sense in which it actually resembled the pandemic. At the time of the first lockdown in 2020, no one imagined that the pandemic would continue to restrict our lives so seriously for all of two years. Initially, we expected it to be over within weeks. Similarly, my project began as a quite modest one. But it grew and grew, keeping pace as it were with the ongoing course of the pandemic, until, early in 2022, I realized it would need to be published as two large volumes. At this point the publishers, who seemed entirely happy with the monstrous growth of the work, agreed that they would publish the first volume whenever it was ready without waiting for volume 2, which could be published later. At that stage I had written a great deal of both volumes, including about 80 percent of volume 2, but I decided the priority now was to complete volume 1 and make it ready for publication. So in the early part of the year—up to my visit to Alnmouth in March—I was working very hard on volume 1. When I left home for Alnmouth, there was one substantial chapter I had started but not been able to finish. Completing that chapter and writing the conclusion to the volume would be easily doable before Easter.

Of course, the sudden degeneration of my eyesight threw that in doubt. But just a week after my first visit to the eye clinic, in a state of great anxiety about my eyesight, I wrote to friends that "whatever happens, I am determined to get [volume 1] to the publishers before Easter. I have to work while I still can." It was difficult. I had to hold every book I needed to consult close to my eyes, not easy when turning the pages of big reference books or finding the exact place in a book where the requisite information or opinion is located. But I got that chapter and the conclusion to the volume finished and to the publisher on April 28, less than two weeks after Easter.

I thought that my vocation to research and to write was going to be more difficult, but I had no intention of abandoning it. Apart from volume 2 of this pandemic project, I also had any number of unfinished projects on which I had done much work. These were not projects someone else could finish. So I began to explore ways of being able to read books with much reduced eyesight.

I think my determination to continue with my work, whatever the difficulties, must be what more than one of my friends commended as my "fortitude." I prefer to speak of "vigorous faith," the term I brought with me from Alnmouth, because it was a matter of relying on God for the ability to continue with the vocation I understood he had given me and not withdrawn.

In the weeks following my first eye injection on April 5, it seemed to be having its expected effect of stabilizing the condition of my eye. At first I was buoyed up by an overwhelming sense of gratitude to God for the fact that I could still read, even though my ability to read was now restricted. The period of acute anxiety seemed to have come to an end, though I knew there could be no guarantee that my eye would not deteriorate further.

I began to think about the technological aids that are available for making the most of "low vision" (as I now knew my condition is called). What gave me the most hope were the desktop electronic magnifiers that enable one to read books. Various suppliers advertise such devices online, but ordering such a thing online without seeing or trying it would be foolish. It seemed frustratingly difficult to get to see any of them. One supplier I proposed visiting said they did not keep them in stock. The Cambridge charity for the blind—CamSight—has a demonstration center where they have a wide range of equipment useful to people with low vision, but this was still closed because of Covid and would not reopen until late May or June. The RNIB (Royal National Institute for Blind People) has a shop in London that was also closed for Covid, but I arranged an individual visit there. This proved disappointing because I was shown two small magnifiers (I bought one of these later) but not the big ones I was really wanting to see. Eventually, a friend who is well known to CamSight interceded for me, and they agreed to loan me one. When it finally arrived in my home on May 5, I was delighted to find how effective it was. I could read papers and books, turn the pages, refer back and forth within a book, move about on a page with great ease—all the time with the print magnified on a screen in very clear form and displayed in different modes, such as white on black or black on yellow, for easier reading.

Some weeks previously, it had felt as though my access to the whole world of books had been barred, the door slammed in my face, leaving me able only to peer in through frosted glass. But now the door had been flung open again and I was allowed back in. The Clear View C Desktop Magnifier had given me back my books.

9

Providence

A Theological Reflection

Whenever we tell stories to make some sense of our life, or the
life of the world, providence is almost always the ghost-writer.

—Vernon White, *Purpose and Providence*

"We know that all things work together for good for those
who love God" (Rom. 8:28).[1] These words from the New
Testament sank deep into my consciousness long ago—I do not
remember when, but probably during my student days. What
they express (known as the doctrine of special providence) is
even more fundamental to the way I have lived and understood
the Christian life throughout my adult life. I do not remember
actually bringing these words to mind during the experiences

1. This is the most familiar translation, found, e.g., in the NRSV. Another
reading is "God makes all things work together for good" or "in all things God
works for good."

narrated in this book, but I took for granted throughout that
I live within God's loving care and that God is at work in the
events of my life. I never doubted that whatever happened to
me would be within God's loving purpose for me.

The word *providence* derives from the Latin verb *providere*,
meaning "to see beforehand, to have foresight." (The English
words *provide* and *provision* also derive from this Latin word.)
Providence refers to God's beneficent government of the world
through his wisdom and foreknowledge. Traditionally, theology
has distinguished between general providence and special providence. The former refers to the way God constantly upholds
the existence and order of the whole of the creation. The latter
refers to the way he provides for his people in particular ways,
acting in the events of their lives to protect and to care for them,
with their ultimate good in view.

When I taught at the University of Manchester, Professor
Richard Hanson, who was then the professor of theology, was
in the habit of walking around the university campus holding an
open book and apparently absorbed in reading it. The fact that
he came to no harm, never tripping or bumping into anything
or anyone, I used to say was a shining example of the doctrine
of special providence. That was in the days before smartphones.
Nowadays we often see people who are seemingly entrusting
their care to special providence while they walk around with
eyes fixed on their phones. I have sometimes bumped into
them, which may suggest that God is not too concerned about
enabling them to do this with impunity.

The two forms of providence are not unrelated. Special
providence is really an aspect of the way God is constantly
active in his creation, upholding it in general in ways that aim
for its good and acting in specific ways in and around the lives
of individuals and groups for their good. From now on I shall
call special providence simply "providence," since it is God's

loving care for me in the events of my life that is my present subject.

It has always seemed to me that belief in providence is essential to the Christian vision of life. Much prayer presupposes that God can and will act to bring about what he is asked. For example, the petition in the Lord's Prayer, "Give us today our daily bread," makes sense only if we believe that God has some control or influence over the way we are provided with the basic necessities of life. The petition is not a pious wish but an appeal to God's power to do specific things in the world. Normally, of course, our daily bread reaches us through identifiable human means that intervene between the wheat field and the table. But if this kind of prayer is valid, these human means do not exclude the action of God. I know that some readers will immediately find this problematic. In fact, providence seems to me one of those Christian beliefs that is essential in the living and practice of the Christian faith but which is really puzzling when one sits back and thinks about it. So it is worth taking some time to consider why it is that people today may find providence a difficult belief. I say "today" deliberately, because I think there are reasons why modern people, including modern Christians, may find providence a whole lot more problematic than people in the past did. I shall discuss four such reasons.

The first is scientific determinism. Many scientists have been so impressed by the way science has revealed the tight relationship of cause and effect in natural processes that they claim that everything that happens in the world is determined by the operation of inflexible laws of nature. Everything follows inevitably from its preceding cause. There is no such thing as chance. (Albert Einstein famously said that God does not throw dice.) Our human sense of freedom to choose and to act without compulsion is ultimately illusory. It should be said at once that science has not proved that determinism is true. It is really a *belief* about the world that seems plausible to those who observe that much of what happens in the natural world seems to be the predictable result of identifiable causes. But science itself, in the form of subatomic physics, seems to have shown that deep in the material nature of things there is fundamental unpredictability. Furthermore, many of us are not willing to think that human freedom is an illusion. The phenomenon of consciousness needs to be taken seriously as an emergent phenomenon of the world that is not reducible to the mechanical operation of the laws of physics. John Polkinghorne, as expert a physicist as he was a theologian, writes of "a flexibility within the open process of the universe which encourages us to think that [the providential activity of God] is a coherent possibility."[2]

This is not the place to pursue these vitally important issues. What I wish to point out is that if the world is actually open to the exercise of human freedom, then it is hard to see why it should not also be open to the exercise of the freedom of God, its Creator. Some of the patterns we observe in the texture of reality are woven by the operation of the laws of nature, but there are other threads interwoven with them that would make a big difference to the whole picture, were we able to see it.

Owing to the influence of a deterministic view of the natural world, some Christians seem to think that God can act in the world only through the activity of humans. They presuppose human freedom and our ability to relate to God through our mental processes. God can influence us but not the rest of reality independently of us. (I think this view is not uncommon. I once asked a class of about fifteen students studying theology what they thought about this, and they all agreed that God acts in the world only through humans.) But we should note that

2. John Polkinghorne, *Science and Providence: God's Interaction with the World* (London: SPCK, 1989), 17.

scientific determinism would make it just as difficult to conceive of God influencing individual humans as it is to think of God influencing the course of events in the natural world. A closed universe is closed to God's activity in relation to human minds just as much as it closed to any other sort of divine activity. But if we suppose that human decisions and actions are free and able to affect the course of the world to some degree (since human freedom is, of course, limited), it is entirely conceivable that God is also free to do so. Indeed, if God is really God, we can hardly conceive of him as less free than human beings.

The theological bedrock is that God gives his creation existence not just once at its beginning, but constantly. He continuously holds it in being. Without God's action in upholding it, creation would revert at once to nothingness. This means that God also sustains every part of creation in its regular, lawlike activity. Effects follow from causes because God constantly enables them to do so. If this is the case, then it is conceivable that God is also able to make a difference to the way things turn out. He acts in, with, and alongside the lawlike operation of cause and effect. Scientific investigation is so constructed that it observes only the regularities, not the larger shaping of them into providential patterns of special divine activity. Miracles, perhaps, are not so completely out of accord with the rest of the way the world works. They are those rare (or perhaps, we may one day realize, not so rare) occasions when God, instead of enabling the regular sequence of cause and effect, interrupts it so that something different happens. Science has no possible way of demonstrating that this never happens.

I am not here concerned with miracles, but with the ordinary way in which God is always at work within the texture of reality that is otherwise formed by the operations of natural laws, by the effects of human freedom, and also, I think we should add, by mere chance. None of these, enabled by God, excludes his own freedom to act and to influence. We might be helped here by the notion of sufficient cause. A particular factor may be a necessary cause of some event, but it may not be a sufficient cause. Historians are much more familiar than scientists with this situation. Many causes contributed, for example, to the outbreak of the Second World War. Some were big social and economic causes; others were the decisions certain powerful individuals made, when they could have decided otherwise. Natural as well as human factors could have played a part. The coincidental confluence of different factors was also significant. Many different sorts of causes came together, and none is sufficient to explain the outbreak of war. A historian could never be confident that he or she had exhaustively explained what happened. The world is simply too complex for that. Specific causes may be real without being sufficient to explain what happened. The texture of history is loosely, not tightly, woven, and it is not possible, other than for a priori reasons, to deny that God also is active in the course of historical events.

We could surely apply the same consideration to the events of our personal lives. What happens in and around us, what influences us and what influence we have—the web of interactions is surely very complex. We can tell the story differently by focusing on different causes, different aspects, different lines of development, and these different versions of the story may well be complementary, not contradictory. We can never be sure we have *sufficiently* explained why things turned out the way they did. Therefore, we cannot, other than for a priori reasons, exclude the activity of God in, with, and alongside the many other factors. Once we begin to think within this real complexity of real events, the simple model of scientific determinism, inferred from the observation of physical processes, must come to seem far too simple. There is no good reason to suppose that all the complexity of human life is reducible to the level of laws of physics.

I have suggested that we think of God working in, with, and alongside the agency of creatures. Here I differ from a form of theological response to scientific determinism that in effect replaces it with a theological determinism. This view would propose that behind all secondary causes investigated by scientists and historians, God is the primary cause of everything. Theological determinism has had a strong influence in the Christian tradition, both Catholic and Protestant. (It is a mistake to think of it purely as Calvinism.) At first sight, its picture of God as the all-powerful ruler of the universe who determines everything that happens may look biblical. But its most obvious flaw lies in the problem of evil. If God determines everything, then it is very hard to maintain an adequate distinction between evil, which he opposes, and good, which he promotes. In the modern period it has become very common for Christian theologians and other Christians to vindicate the goodness of God by ascribing evil to human freedom (and perhaps also the freedom of supernatural agents and of the natural world). God is then said to permit evil, for the sake of the eventual achievement of the ultimate good of creation. Theological determinism cannot make this distinction between what God permits and what he actively promotes.

God is, of course, the power over everything. He is all-powerful and could determine all the events in his creation. However, it need not follow that he does so. Rather, God's creation of the world gives it not only existence but also the ability to be itself. I am not inclined to think of this as a kind of self-abnegation by God, as some have advocated. Rather, God's creation of a world that can develop in part through its own free agency (which I do not limit to humans) is precisely an exercise of his creative power. In order to create the sort of world he values, God can and does choose to create this kind of world. But he does not withdraw from it like the deistic clockmaker. He not only upholds it in being but also is actively engaged with it in all its aspects. Creatures have their own genuine agency, appropriate to their various natures, but because this is creaturely agency, it is limited. It is never the sufficient cause of anything. God engages with it in a no doubt incalculable range of different ways. He acts in, with, and alongside creaturely agencies. He permits evil, but he also works actively to restrain and to overcome evil. He promotes goodness and engages humans in the cosmic task of bringing the whole creation to its ultimate good. The way to this ultimate good is foreseen and planned by God, but it is not wholly determined. Yet the power of his love at work in the creation guarantees that the ultimate goal will be achieved.

This is an approach that gives providence an overriding role in human affairs without canceling the reality of creaturely agency and its effects. What is provided for us by God's loving providence will be the best that can be provided in the circumstances, not necessarily the best that might be available in a quite different kind of world from this.

A second reason for finding providence a problematic concept today is just as modern as scientific determinism, but curiously contradictory in that it makes much of the human freedom that scientific determinism denies. This second reason is the characteristically modern sense of the controllability of the world by humans. The German sociologist Hartmut Rosa, in his book *The Uncontrollability of the World*, argues that a major change in the human relationship to the world has come about in the modern period. There have always been two aspects to how humans relate to the world. On the one hand, it is characteristic of humans to seek and to acquire some degree of control over the world, but on the other hand, humans recognize and respond appropriately to the fact that what happens is largely outside human control. But in the modern period, partly as a result of the success of science and technology, control has become the dominant form of human approach to the world. "Everything that appears to us must be known, mastered, conquered, made useful."[3] An overriding cultural trend in this direction in science, technology, politics, economics, and other fields means that most people now relate to the world around them as something to be controlled. Rosa is clear that control is a natural and necessary aspect of the human approach to the world, but when everything becomes manageable and predictable, the world loses much of its magic and meaning. Some have called this the disenchantment of the world.

What is especially lost is what he calls "resonance," which occurs when the uncontrollable "speaks" to us in some way, and we respond and are affected and are transformed in ways that are not predictable. We do not merely appropriate the world but allow an open-ended encounter with an unpredictable other. Resonance (which can be illustrated in experiences such as responses to art or nature) cannot occur if the human person relates to the world only by way of mastery and control. Similarly, it cannot be achieved by some calculable method.

It will be helpful for us to illustrate this in terms of personal life. Modern people characteristically want to be in control of their lives, to choose their own goals, and to set out to achieve them. An illustration of this is the popularity of dating apps, which allow someone to specify in detail the sort of person they want to meet, the sort of person they already know or

3. Hartmut Rosa, *The Uncontrollability of the World*, trans. James C. Wagner (Cambridge: Polity, 2020).

think they know will be compatible and attractive. The attempt is to make romance controllable and predictable. But what is ruled out is the adventure of falling in love with an unlikely person, and all the unexpected enhancements of life that may follow. The attempt to control all aspects of life deprives life of its surprises and its unexpectedly transformative encounters. When someone knows exactly what they want from experiences such as social life or travel or even having children and enters such experiences with the intention of achieving that, these experiences are drained of life, because it is responsiveness to the uncontrollable that gives life much of its meaning. Predictability is not only dull; it is deadening.

Rosa argues that, paradoxically, modern humanity's apparently extensive achievement of control over the world has resulted in greater unpredictability, which modern humanity, addicted to control, finds threatening. The environmental crisis is an obvious example. But in the sphere of personal life, we may think of the control people have over the course of their own lives. In the not too distant past, for example, most people had a quite limited choice of occupation and could expect to stay in that occupation for life. Modern people in Western societies, where freedom to choose is highly valued, typically have a wide range of career options available to them. This gives them, in theory at least, much more control over their lives. But it also opens up a much more unpredictable future than their ancestors had. Few people are in jobs for life. Being able to move around as one chooses in the marketplace of employment may seem to give people more control over their lives, but it goes along with huge elements of unpredictability in the workings of the modern economy.

It is noteworthy that Rosa himself takes the idea of the Jewish and Christian God (writing sociology, he is naturally not committed to the reality of God) as a kind of model of uncontrollability. God is the ultimately uncontrollable one. Rosa makes the insightful observation that prayer is not, as magic is, an attempt to manage supernatural power and engineer outcomes. God is not accessible to control, but he is accessible in relationship that involves receptivity, responsiveness, and transformation. Relationship with God is not achieved but experienced as gift bestowed on us or happening to us.[4] It is starkly unlike modern humanity's desire to gain and to exercise control over reality.

Rosa does not suggest, but it seems to me likely, that the so-called death of God, meaning the widespread loss of an awareness of God in modern culture, has a lot to do with the way modern humanity approaches the world as controllable. It is due not so much to the actual extent to which control over the world has been achieved by science and technology as to the attitude of management, mastery, and predictability that has come to dominate people's approach to the world. Imagining we have extensive control over the world leaves little room for God. Approaching every aspect of life with the desire to control makes the very idea of God undesirable. For God is the ultimately uncontrollable one whom we can recognize as active in the world only if we are open to the significance of what simply happens to us or is simply given to us, entirely beyond our control.

A third reason for finding providence a problematic concept today is the problem of innocent suffering. This is by no means just a modern phenomenon. It is already powerfully presented in the book of Job in the Old Testament. But in the modern period it does seem to have become a dominant objection to

4. Rosa, *Uncontrollability of the World*, 58–60.

religious belief. When people who do not believe or practice a religion are asked why, they regularly say that a good God would not permit all the suffering that exists in the world. Of course, many of these people may not have thought seriously about faith in God at all and are simply citing what is commonly said without any deep concern with the problem of suffering. It is certainly notable that the problem is more often raised as a reason for not believing by people who are relatively affluent and comfortable than by people who are undergoing severe suffering. At the time of the Boxing Day tsunami in 2004, one of the worst natural disasters of recent times, which devastated parts of Indonesia, armchair commentators in the Western media asked, "How can anyone believe in God after this?" But I recall seeing people on the spot, who had lost everything, interviewed on the news. They said that it was only their faith in God, as Muslims, that enabled them to keep going. They had a strong belief in providence that sustained them in extreme circumstances that might otherwise have defeated them. Many similar examples, including Jewish believers in the Nazi death camps, could easily be provided.

However, this cannot excuse us from taking the prevalence of evil and suffering in the world as a serious matter for belief in the loving and all-powerful God of Christian faith. The subject has, of course, been extensively examined and debated and has many aspects. We cannot discuss it here at any length. I merely offer a few considerations. First, because God is goodness itself, we must distinguish God's relationships to good and evil in the world. God initiates and promotes good. He permits evil but restrains it, inspires opposition to it, and works for a redemptive outcome.

Second, although Christians must believe that God is at work throughout his creation, we cannot reasonably expect to understand his purpose in all the innumerable events of nature and history in their vast complexity. In many ways, providence is a secretive process we cannot hope to fathom, at least before the end of history. There is a proper degree of agnosticism involved in faith in the God who utterly transcends his creation.

Third, the way we understand events depends on the context in which we view them, and it changes as that context broadens. Thus, it is possible, in an individual life, for events that seem nothing but tragic at the time to acquire good outcomes when seen in a later perspective. I recently read about a journalist who had a very troubled childhood, shunted from one unsatisfactory foster home to another. But as a young man, he was grateful for this experience, without which he would not have had the insight into the deprived and difficult lives he wanted to write about.

Fourth, insofar as we have been given insight into the purposes of God in the world, it is found in the biblical metanarrative, the overall story the Bible tells about God and the world, stretching from creation to the new creation and focused on the story of Jesus—his life, death, resurrection, and future. It offers many perspectives on the way. God deals with evil, including the perplexity of Job and the protests of the psalmists. But at its heart is the cross, where God himself suffers in solidarity with his whole creation and its manifold plight. This proves to be the unexpected way in which God delivers creation from evil and prepares it for eternity, when he "will wipe every tear from their eyes" (Rev. 21:4). Insofar as we are able to identify God's purposes at work in the world, the biblical metanarrative and the story of Jesus in particular are the master keys.

Finally, a Christian response to evil and suffering must include not only faith but also love and hope. We do not have an explanation for evil that allows us to justify it as God's will and so to simply accept it. Evil is what God opposes, and so we align ourselves with God's loving purpose to overcome it. We must love all who suffer, and we hope for the ultimate redemption of the whole creation. Only then will the total and final context in which all events are understood be available.

Finally, a fourth consideration that for some people makes it hard to believe in special providence has to do with the immensity of the universe as we now perceive it. If God created and manages this whole vast creation (even supposing there is only one universe), is it plausible that he micromanages the details of our daily lives? In fact, this is not a particularly modern question. The author of Psalm 8 already observed how insignificant human beings seem in the context of the heavens, even in the worldview of the ancient Near East. He marveled that God should interest himself in humans, but firmly believed that he did and wondered at the generous grace of such a God. Our apparent insignificance in the vast universe can be a cause not for supposing that God is unlikely to be concerned for us but for grateful amazement at the fact that he is.

Does the mere size of this planet in comparison with the unimaginable extent of the universe necessarily make it unimportant in the eyes of the Creator of all? In fact, it is a mistake to suppose that relative size in any way correlates with relative importance. Very small things can be much more important than very big things. For example, in terms of their effect in human history, short texts such as the Christian creeds and *The Communist Manifesto* have been far more important than the vast majority of huge tomes. It is entirely conceivable that human beings are far more important to God than many a galaxy.

Such arguments will not convince those who find it hard to imagine how God could possibly have, as it were, a mental grasp of everything that is happening all the time throughout

the vast reaches of the universe and down to the smallest subatomic particles and the merest trace of a thought in a human
mind. This difficulty arises from confining God to the analogy
of a human mind or, perhaps, a supercomputer. God is not
just much "bigger" than either of those; he is utterly "other"
than them. We cannot help thinking of God as perceiving and
understanding things the way we do. But this is a human analogy that the true God transcends. When we speak of God's
omniscience, we mean more than that what he knows is not
limited, as our knowledge is. We mean that he transcends all
the limitations of created intelligence. A human mind cannot
hold very many things in its consciousness at once. Not so for
God. It is not that God's mind has a much greater capacity. For
God, knowing everything about everything is not in any way
difficult or problematic. In this and in so many other ways,
we cannot imagine what it is like for God to be God. Rather,
we know, without being able to imagine it, that we are finite
creatures and that God is not. We can truly know God by the
analogies with his creatures that he gives us, but only if we also
recognize that he is incomprehensibly other than creatures.
Simply because God is God and not human, as Jesus said, he
knows the number of the hairs on every human head just as
easily as, according to the psalmist, he knows the number of
the stars in the universe.[5]

I have offered, all too briefly, a general *apologia* for the notion of providence, but since this book is about my experience
of living within God's providential care, I should like to return
to the quotation from Paul's Letter to the Romans with which
I began this chapter: "We know that all things work together
for good for those who love God" (Rom. 8:28). Undoubtedly,
the background to Paul's thought here is a general conviction of

5. Matt. 10:30; Luke 12:7; Ps. 147:4.

God's governance of the world and its history, such as he would have learned from the Hebrew Scriptures, but he is concerned with the implication for his readers, "those who love God." We need not suppose, on the basis of these words, that God's good purpose does not extend to those who do not love God. Paul would have said that God's purpose, as seen in the events of Jesus's life, death, and resurrection, was that all people should come to know God's love and to respond in love for God. All human life is richly blessed by God, but since loving God is the fulfillment for which all people have been created, their ultimate "good" must include their coming to love God.

What Paul means by "good" is the ultimate good that those who love God will attain in the new creation, when God will achieve the ultimate good of his whole creation. This is clear from the context, in which verse 28 follows verses 18–25. In that passage Paul is concerned with the contrast between "the sufferings of the present time" and "the glory about to be revealed to us" (Rom. 8:18). At the present time, believers are afflicted with the difficulties and sufferings that are inseparable from life in this world, but they have the sure hope of "glory" when the whole creation is renewed. So when Paul says that "all things work together for good," he does not mean that providence will ensure that "those who love God" will have trouble-free lives. He means that whatever happens to them will in the end lead to their ultimate "good."

This is developed later in the chapter, where God's love for us takes priority over our love for God: "Who will separate us from the love of Christ? Will hardship, or distress, or persecution, or famine, or nakedness, or peril, or sword?" (Rom. 8:35). This catalog of troubles may well reflect Paul's own experience. He had suffered most of them in the course of his apostolic labors and had found for himself that they did not separate him from the love of God as he had come to know it in Jesus

Christ. Paul's writing then becomes lyrical as he accumulates a long series of even more daunting forms of opposition that might be barriers to God's love for his people, beginning with death and ending with "anything else in all creation" (8:39).

As an interpretation of providence, this passage is notable for its focus on Jesus Christ (Rom. 8:34, 35, 39). The way God works in "all things" for the ultimate "good" of those he loves and who love him is Christ-shaped. It has the contours of the cross and the resurrection. Therefore, sufferings, contradictions, and difficulties, far from being excluded, are the expected context in which God's love will be experienced and his purpose worked out. There is a kind of solidarity between the passion of Jesus and the sufferings of those who trust in him. The love of God for the world, which Jesus embraced and implemented when he went to his death on the cross, reaches above all those who embrace that love as followers of Jesus. Absolutely nothing at all "will be able to separate us from the love of God in Christ Jesus our Lord" (8:39).

I have been privileged to know just one centenarian. Brother Herbert Kaden, a Benedictine monk, died recently at the age of 101. Several weeks previously, when he seemed hale and hearty, I asked him if from his long life he was able to distill any spiritual advice. He said he could do so in just one word: *accept*. He instanced, as an example, the time when, in his thirties, he was "certified" and had to spend five months in a mental hospital against his will. He had been in a state of some mental disturbance but years later was still sure that he would have been better off recovering at home. He wrote that the "first weeks in the hospital were terrible." But with the arrival of spring, he slowly realized that "all was not wrong—that there was a purpose in my being in that hospital. It was after all,

God's will." This made the rest of his time there more tolerable, even though he was subjected to insulin treatment and ECT (electroconvulsive therapy), treatments that are now regarded as misguided. To some people they were harmful, "but not," he recalled, "to me, thank God, for gradually I began to improve."[6] It is important to realize that he was referring to a situation he had no power to change. When I asked, he agreed with me that his watchword, *accept*, should not apply to situations that one has the ability to ameliorate or even to transform.

I am reminded of Paul's mysterious "thorn in the flesh," which may well have been recurrent migraines. He says that "three times I appealed to the Lord about this, that it would leave me, but he said to me, 'My grace is sufficient for you, for my power is made perfect in weakness'" (2 Cor. 12:8–9). Paul came to see that it was good for him to accept this "weakness," along with other such weaknesses, because they made it evident that the "power" at work in his apostolic ministry was God's, not an ability of his own of which he could boast (12:7–10). Whether or not he was aware of it, Paul was following the Jesus of Gethsemane.

Accepting what happens to us as God's will is not the same as resigning ourselves to inevitable fate. It differs from fatalism because we know that, within God's providential care, God is calling us to participate with him in his purposes for ourselves and for others. He is acting not only for us but also with us. Ideally, we will not just passively accept but actively affirm God's will for us (as Brother Herbert did in the mental hospital), though it is not wrong to struggle with circumstances and cry out to God in bewilderment, as the psalmists often do. If we are able to identify and affirm God's will for us, then we also know that God wants us to collaborate with him through

6. Brother Herbert Kaden, *Some Memories of My Life* (n.p.: privately printed, 2008), 57–58.

prayer and action, in whatever ways might be appropriate. We do what we can in the direction of what, as far as we are able to tell, is God's purpose.

With this kind of awareness of providence, we shall be able to avoid the temptation of exaggerating the power of our own agency. We are never in a position single-handedly and infallibly to achieve an outcome. Attendant circumstances always make a difference. We do not even fully control our own psychological states or perceptions or motivations. We may play a greater or a lesser role in an outcome, but we are never in control. Awareness of providence can keep us from the many dangers of overreaching. On the other hand, it should not deincentivize us, as though we were helpless to act at all. Quite the opposite, it will give us the confidence that if we are seeking God's will, God will prosper our action. He can make more of what we do than we can make of it ourselves.

Although I did not think about it at the time, the way I applied myself to researching and getting electronic aids for low vision in the period after my first eye injection was an attempt to exert some control over what was happening to me. I was struggling to find a way through what seemed to me the encroaching darkness of a life in which I might have real difficulty reading. Of course, it also gave me something purposeful to do in a period of anxious waiting. It was not inconsistent with trusting that God was working out his loving purpose for me. I was holding on to my conviction that my vocation, as I understood it, was still my calling from God. The electronic aids encouraged me to think I would be able to continue that, even if it became more difficult.

As I stated before, God is the ultimately uncontrollable one. Trusting in his providential care does not mean that we can count on a particular outcome, only that he will in the end achieve his good purposes for us. We should not be so self-centered as to forget that God's purposes in the world go way beyond ourselves. That was the lesson Job had to learn. Collaborating with God in those wider purposes means accepting outcomes that we would not have wished for ourselves. At times his providence may seem utterly opaque to us. But even as we cry, "Why? Why?" in bewilderment, we can still trust that his love for us has not diminished and will ensure our ultimate good.

Belief in providence may be difficult, but it is also productive of thanksgiving. It enables us in retrospect, whether that be at the end of a day or years later, to see what God has been doing in our lives and to be grateful.

10

The Story, Part 4

The Blurred Cross

I bind unto myself today
The power of God to hold and lead,
His eye to watch, his might to stay,
His ear to hearken to my need.

— "St. Patrick's Breastplate"

At the morning service in St. Mark's Church, Newnham, I usually sit in a pew near the back. It is a fairly small church, and there are usually between fifty and a hundred people in the congregation. I know most of them. I like to sit in the back because from there I can see and recognize many of the people I know. I really value being able to see that I am worshiping with all those people I know and love. But on Sunday, April 24, 2022, about three weeks after my first eye injection, this joy turned to sadness. Those people were fading out of my vision. I could still identify many as familiar shapes sitting in their usual places. But they were very blurred. Even Andrew, our curate, sitting at the other end of the pew I was in, was indistinct. The visiting preacher was a mere blur in the pulpit, and the service leader I knew only by his near-disembodied voice. This was one of the occasions when I realized just how cloudy my sight in my left eye had become.

This increasing cloudiness showed me that the injection had not stabilized the condition of my eye. It was continuing to deteriorate. The distortion of my vision (straight lines seen as wavy) remained the same, but this new phenomenon of cloudy vision was a development that worried me. I wondered if it was actually an effect of the injection. The cloudiness came home to me again when I attempted some gardening. In bright sunshine I couldn't see clearly enough the plants I was handling. Visiting a friend's garden, I realized I couldn't, without going close, distinguish forget-me-nots from bluebells. They were a pretty but unidentifiable blue blur. In my journal I considered that I might need to employ someone to look after my small back garden and sadly remarked "how much my life is changing." Not just reading and work but even a simple activity like gardening, which I had always enjoyed, was being taken from me.

These observations were especially worrying because I believed that the injections could not reverse any deterioration in my sight, only prevent it from going further. I assumed that the cloudiness would therefore be permanent. Moreover, it was increasing while I waited for the second injection. Then I observed a small, faint patch of blurriness at the center of my vision in my left eye. To me it resembled the large circle of blurriness at the center of my vision in my right eye, except that the latter was dark and the former was light. It suggested to me that my left eye was now going the way of my right eye and that the process was now out of control. The small, faint patch would likely become a larger, dark one before it could be treated, as had been the case with my right eye.

I knew that the second injection ought to be a month after the first, but the end of that month was approaching and I had not received notification from the hospital of a date for the injection. So I phoned the eye clinic. I was lucky, on this occasion, to have my call answered by a human being. A helpful voice told me that an appointment had been made for me for the injection on May 26—that is, seven weeks after the first injection. This was why I hadn't yet received notification of it. I said, with deliberate lack of pushy assertiveness (usually counterproductive), that although I didn't pretend to understand these things, I thought that the injections were supposed to be four weeks apart. The helpful man consulted his information and found that there was an open slot, owing to a cancellation, on May 11. (What had happened, of course, was that the appointment had been made by the hospital bureaucracy, not by Mr. K, the consultant, who had arranged the first injection. No doubt, I had simply been placed in a queue. No consideration was given to whether it was important that the second injection follow the first after no more than the recommended interval.)

I then explained to the man on the phone that I was concerned about the way my eyesight was now deteriorating. I wondered whether I might speak to Mr. K about it on the phone. (Had this been possible, it might have spared me a great deal of anxiety. But it is impossible to speak to any of the doctors at the eye clinic on the phone. The bureaucracy protects them from any such intrusion. One of the things that made my whole experience with the eye clinic so stressful and distressing was that one couldn't talk to anyone except during the severely rationed and restricted appointments. As will be clear, these would prove to be not only unhelpful but also seriously misleading and detrimental. A telephone call with someone who really knew their stuff would have made a huge difference.)

The helpful man on the phone made an appointment for me to see a junior doctor the following morning. I had the usual eye scan, and Dr. A, after examining my eyes and looking at the scan, said he could see no sign of further deterioration. As for my observation of the patch of blur in the center of my vision, he said that the mind can play tricks on one. There seemed nothing more I could do except wait two more weeks for the second injection, scheduled now for May 11. I asked Dr. A if I could phone the eye clinic if I observed any further deterioration in my eye. He said yes but only if there was something really substantial. I took him to mean: not something like this imaginary matter you have wasted my time with today. I wrote in my journal that "the worst thing about dealing with the hospital has been my almost desperate sense of urgency and their lack of it."

In the following days, my mood swung between elation and anxiety. The elation was due to technology. I was so impressed by the electronic magnifier that I went to Heffers bookshop and bought a new book about Rilke's poetry. I felt so happy that I would actually be able to read it. At the same time I reflected that, if my eyesight continued to deteriorate, I would have difficulty reading even with the aid of the magnifier. The same evening I noticed I could not see properly the piece of fish I cooked for my evening meal. I also had great difficulty clipping my toenails. However much I contorted myself and put my feet into the best available light, I could not see my toenails. I wrote, "Lord, I know that you will get me through all this. . . . I know that the way of the cross may get much harder. My vocation may be more difficult than I ever expected. I have had fifteen really, really *good* years here [in Newnham]. I have so much to thank God for. Just please, please don't let me lose the ability to read with some degree of ease and pleasure."

The blot in the center of my vision in my left eye was certainly not a trick of my imagination. I could see it as a patch of blur when I watched television, obscuring every face I looked at. Most worryingly, I could see it as a blind spot when I read print, even using the magnifier, with its power to clarify as well as enlarge. A small bit of each letter was missing in my sight of it. I could still read, but it was laborious. But after what Dr. A had said, I did not feel able to contact the eye clinic. It was agonizing, but I waited until May 11. Quite often I prayed my personal version of lines from "St. Patrick's Breastplate":

> Christ, embrace me,
> Christ, enfold me,
> Christ, with your strong
> love uphold me.

The verse ("Christ be with me . . .") was in my mind as I waited in the now familiar waiting room with its spaced chairs and anxious (or so I imagined), silent patients on the morning of May 11. During that wait I composed another prayer, which was, oddly, inspired by the machine that scanned my eyes. For the eye to be looking in the right direction for each scan, I was asked to focus on a small blue cross that lit up in the darkness. Back in my seat, I thought:

> The cross of Christ to save and bless me,
> the cross of Christ to lead and summon me.

The cross represents both the amazing grace of God in our lives and also the path of discipleship on which we are called to follow Christ. I wanted to be conscious of both aspects at this critical moment in my life.

I knew that I was to see a junior doctor. (To see a consultant more than once would be unthinkable.) The nurse had referred to him by his first name, as they often do. When a doctor emerged from one of the consulting rooms and spoke my name, I was shocked to see that it was Dr. A. (I had not known his first name.) "I'm Dr. A. I saw you last time you were here," he said unnecessarily. "You know that we can't give injections less than four weeks apart," he added. He made the same point again later, which puzzled me at the time. I thought he must be talking about my third injection, still to come. I realized later that he was excusing himself for not having done anything when I last came to see him. Even if he had observed something wrong, he meant, he could not have done anything about it before now. Had I been alert to his meaning, I could have pointed out that actually it was now five weeks since I had the first injection. But it is a feature of this kind of medical consultation that the patient, feeling acutely anxious, is not able to think with optimal sharpness.

I think I told him something about the present condition of my eye as I saw it. He examined my eye, rather cursorily it seemed to me. ("Look up, look right, look down, look left.") Then he said, "Okay. You have an appointment booked for the next injection in four weeks' time. We'll see how you're getting on then." That would have been the end of the consultation as far as he was concerned. I was staggered. Surely the whole point of a consultation was to inform me how he assessed the state of my eye at this point, in light of the scan and his own examination of it.

I said, "But what do you see in the scan?"

Dr. A: "There is some activity in the eye."
Me: "What does that mean?"

Dr. A: "That's what we call it: activity."

Me: "But what does that *mean*?"

Dr. A: "There is some liquid."

Me: "What sort of liquid? Blood?"

Dr. A: "No, not blood. Liquid."

I found this exchange stupefying. Why did I have to drag this minimal information out of him, almost word by word, like blood out of a stone? I tried to think what else to ask in order to make him say more, but I couldn't think of the right questions. I felt like I was facing a brick wall. I remember putting my head in my hands, trying to think, while he sat silently waiting. I soon realized I would have to go, so I put a parting question to him: "So, this next injection will either stabilize the condition of my eye as it is, or it won't, and the eye will continue to deteriorate?" He said, "Yes." Though this confirmed what I had supposed, hearing it put so bluntly was devastating. He seemed unable even to give me hope that the first of these two alternatives was more likely.

As I left the eye clinic, my mood was about as low as it could be. I felt at the time that I was being shunted through an unfeeling system as quickly as possible. But later on, when I thought about it, it became obvious that Dr. A was not just (or not at all) pressed for time. He was trying to cover up for his incompetence at my first visit, when he should have observed the deterioration that was now very clear in the scan. He was trying to avoid revealing to me the real state of my eye now, because it reflected badly on the way he had treated me two weeks previously. So he didn't want to tell me anything. This was, to say the least, negligent. He was withholding what any patient in such a consultation was entitled to hear: what the scan and the examination revealed. A further serious aspect of Dr. A's incompetence will emerge as this story continues.

I had some time to wait before the eye injection in the afternoon, and so, after getting a coffee, I decided to go to the hospital chapel. I was thinking of it just as somewhere I could sit quietly, but, as it happened, an Anglican communion service was underway. After the parsimonious and uncaring words of Dr. A, I was comforted by the life-giving words of the eucharistic liturgy. With the small congregation of hospital workers and chaplains, I was able to receive communion, and then I stayed after everyone else had left.

Above the altar was a plain black cross that stood out very sharply against a white background. It could have been designed with the needs of people with low vision in mind. In my sight it was blurred. (In addition to the constant cloudiness of my vision in my left eye, it may have still been affected by the eye drops that were put into my eye before it was scanned.) I could see the shape of the cross, but it was blurred. Somehow it seemed a very meaningful symbol of where I was on the way of following the crucified Jesus.

Later (perhaps on the bus home, I forget) I began to compose a poem based on the thought that the eyesight of Jesus, as he hung dying on the cross, would surely have become blurred, smeared with blood and tears that he could not wipe away. I never finished the poem and have only a few jotted lines:

> I think perhaps that when you hung in pain,
> bearing the weight of all this sad world's wrong,
> your vision blurred. Could you distinctly see
> your mother and your friends? . . .
> Through that blur of blood, that cloud of tears and
>   sweat,
> you look with love on all whose sight is dimmed.

I was following through the conviction that Jesus on the cross identified with us all in every aspect of the human plight. Not that he literally suffered all the vast range of different forms of suffering. Of course, that would be impossible. But his extreme wretchedness, suffering one of the most painful ways to die, was a kind of solidarity with all of us in whatever ways we suffer, whether in innocence or guilt. For me at that time, the realization that Jesus may well have literally suffered blurred vision brought home to me the loving solidarity of Jesus with me in what seemed a difficult place to be. Just thinking of the cross can remind us how suffering in the world is huge and extreme. My anxiety about losing the ability to read was trivial by comparison. But the solidarity of the crucified Christ is wide enough to include it nonetheless. That day in the chapel of Addenbrooke's Hospital, his cross addressed me where I was.

In his account of his experience of bereavement, Richard Coles observes that "in moments of intense disturbance our attention is held, not by words but by figures, not fleshed-out characters, but symbols perhaps, the better able to serve as signposts in the unfamiliar and frightening world of bereavement."[1] Though my experience was different, it seems to me that the blurred cross was for me just such a signpost. The biblical term is *sign*, meaning something that conveys a reality much deeper than itself.

The "consultation" with Dr. A stunned me. This was the very darkest moment in this story. I never lost sight of God's presence with me in that darkness, but my experience in the hospital chapel was a fresh assurance of it. The blurred cross was especially what I needed to see because it reminded me of

1. Richard Coles, *The Madness of Grief: A Memoir of Love and Loss* (London: Weidenfeld and Nicolson, 2021), 76.

Jesus Christ's loving solidarity with us at the darkest moment
in his life, his dying. Nothing that can happen to us is beyond
the reach of that loving solidarity of the crucified Christ, God's
own love in its most radical expression.

I remember, that evening, talking with my sister on the phone.
After describing my experience at the hospital, I talked about
what my life would now be like, taking for granted that the
state of my left eye then was how it would remain, unless it
actually deteriorated further. Della asked me about traveling,
and I reflected that public transport would present some challenges, such as not being able to read overhead boards in railway stations, but that these were minor obstacles. People with
low vision are used to finding ways around these, and I had no
intention of giving up traveling, at least within the UK. I also
repeated my determination to carry on with my work, using the
electronic magnifiers. I mentioned that I was thinking of buying
some better torches than I had, to assist my eyesight in various
ways around the house. I mention this conversation to illustrate
that, though I was feeling very low as a result of my meeting with
Dr. A, coming on top of a period of mounting anxiety about the
cloudiness of my vision, I was also drawing on what friends had
called my "fortitude." Some of these plans were sensible ways to
carry on my life, but deep down there was also the determination
to "keep on keeping on," the continuing call of my vocation to
serve God in the way he desired, and that vigorous faith I could
muster only by drawing on God's grace. I realize, of course, that
there was nothing very remarkable about my "fortitude." Others
might have reacted similarly for other reasons and without my
own Christian take on it. In my own experience, however, my
"fortitude" belonged to my walk with God.

That night I slept very badly. Surprisingly perhaps, during
the preceding weeks of high anxiety I had mostly slept well. I
think sleep was a kind of refuge to which my mind gratefully

turned in these difficult times. But this night my sleep was very disturbed. But in the sleep I did get toward morning, I had a remarkably happy dream, from which I woke wishing the dream were the reality of my life and my waking life a dream from which I would awake. As will become apparent, this was not as vain a hope as I supposed.

The following morning I visited Susan, the retired GP, and we sat in the garden discussing my experiences at the hospital. Susan is an unfailingly sympathetic and helpful person. She must have been a wonderful GP, though I can imagine she would always have wanted to give patients more of her time than was available in a busy GP practice. I will mention just two results of our conversation that turned out to be very important. One was that I began to think seriously of switching to private health care. That Susan thought this might be the right way forward was important to me, since Susan is a strong supporter of the National Health Service and not easily persuaded to be critical of health care professionals. I have always been opposed to private health care, mainly because it takes resources away from the NHS. Most of the consultants at the eye clinic at Addenbrooke's seem also to do private work. If they gave all their time to the eye clinic, it might provide a better service. But I felt that the NHS had in this instance let me down so badly, and the matter was so important for me, that I had to think of going private. No doubt I was unlucky to get Dr. A on my case, but it would not be easy or advisable to ask not to be treated by him in the future, and it was unlikely that a consultant, rather than a junior doctor, would see me after the first consultation with Mr. K.

Susan also suggested that she get in touch with a very distinguished ophthalmologist who is married to a relative of hers.

I am not sure whether Professor F, as I will call him, is retired or semiretired, but Susan said she was sure he would be happy to have a talk with me. He is a Christian and, according to Susan, has people with macular degeneration in his church home group. Later Susan contacted him and assured me he would be happy to speak to me on the phone.

On the evening of the next day (Friday), I sent this email to my friends Susan and Mike:

I hardly dare say this but the central vision in my left eye has actually improved! I have just noticed it.

I am sharing it with you both because I think I did explain to you about the small circle of blur that had appeared at the center of my vision—and which I found really scary because it looked like the beginning of what obscures my central vision in my right eye almost completely. It has diminished very considerably, not quite disappeared. But it means that the extra difficulty in reading that I began to have between two weeks and one week ago has gone. I am back to the way I was able to read on this computer screen around the middle of last week—and over the previous two or three weeks.

I did not think the injection was able to do this. Maybe a lot of people's prayers working with the injection!

I will have to look very carefully in the morning to check that I'm not dreaming, and will not tell anyone else until I have done that.

But I'm going to bed praising God.

The following morning I emailed them again:

If I was dreaming then, I'm still dreaming now.

My astonishment, but not my delight and thankfulness to God, was moderated when I then spoke to Professor F on the phone later that day, as this later email to Susan and Mike explains:

> Talking to Susan's ophthalmologist friend, I find that what happened to my eyesight yesterday is what could have been expected to be the result of the injection.
>
> It is beyond frustrating that no one at Addenbrooke's tells you such things. For the continuing treatment of my eye I am going to go private without qualms of conscience, because it is clear that Addenbrooke's are failing people like me. The way I was treated by the doctor I saw on Wednesday seems to me now in calm retrospection utterly shocking. He was just not doing his job.

Professor F could not have been more helpful. He explained carefully what happens to the eye in macular degeneration of the kind I had. He explained that Lucentis, the drug that is injected into the eye, should clear the liquid from the macula that was the cause of the blurring or clouding of vision that I had been experiencing. Dr. A should have been able to tell me that. Instead of leaving me with the prospect of my eyesight remaining as it was or further deteriorating, he should have told me there was a very good chance the injection I was having that afternoon would remove much or all of the clouding of my vision. It would remove the "liquid" on the macula that he had seen on the scan of my eye and had so reluctantly told me was there without making any further comment. It was now perfectly clear that Dr. A was not only negligent but also shockingly incompetent. He must have realized he did not know enough to give me a proper diagnosis and should have called in another doctor to look at my scan and discuss it with me.

Professor F also advised, as Susan had suggested, that I transfer the treatment of my eye to private health care and named some consultants at the Spire Hospital near Cambridge whom he advised were very good ophthalmologists. He confirmed, as I had suspected, that complaining about Dr. A and asking to be treated by another doctor at the eye clinic might be problematic. In the face of complaints, colleagues are liable to close ranks and protect their own.

On Monday morning (May 16), I phoned the Spire Hospital, named the ophthalmologists Professor F had recommended, and asked for an appointment with whichever of them could see me soonest. That turned out to be Mr. O at 12:50 that very day. As it happened, Mr. O was the consultant I had seen once at the eye clinic at Addenbrooke's back in 2015, though I remembered nothing much about him except his name.

Waiting at the Spire Hospital was very different from waiting at Addenbrooke's eye clinic. Here the ophthalmology waiting area was more like the carpeted foyer of a good hotel. There were half a dozen upholstered chairs with arms and never more than that number of patients waiting for their tests and scans before seeing a consultant. I did not sense widespread anxiety as I did at the eye clinic. This may have been an inaccurate guess, but the fact that no one was having to wait very long and that everyone saw a consultant pretty much at the appointed time suggests that it was an accurate one. There was no time for anxiety to accumulate, and the surroundings were reassuring. On a later visit I did witness a man complaining loudly and angrily that his wife had had to wait twenty minutes for a blood test, and I felt like telling him it could be very much longer at Addenbrooke's. But no doubt he felt entitled to what he was paying for and part of that was not having to wait.

It was easy to see at once why people should think private health care worth paying for. Everything spoke "privilege," though only because I could contrast it with the state of nonprivileged health care. But above all there was the sense that the staff had time for you. You were not being shunted through a system under severe pressure. That should have been but was actually far from the reality of the NHS—and this was not only, as I had learned by experience, because of the effects of the pandemic.

A great advantage in transferring the care of my eyes to Mr. O was continuity of care. I would remain his patient and not be passed down to any junior doctor who happened to be available. Moreover, if anything happened to cause me concern, I could readily contact his secretary. All this gave me peace of mind, by contrast with the continual anxiety that being dependent on the eye clinic had caused me for weeks. Of course, I was very fortunate to be able to pay for these advantages, and I felt for those people who could not. If other major health issues arise for me, as doubtless they will, I expect I will turn to the NHS for treatment. But my eyesight is of such wide-ranging importance in my life that I am sure I did the right thing by choosing, in this case, private health care, though only after being shockingly failed by the NHS.

At this meeting with Mr. O and the later one I had at the time of my third eye injection, he took great care to explain the condition of my eye. The contrast with Dr. A could hardly have been greater. As I now understood it, two things had happened to my eye. One was a scar on the macula, which was causing the distortion in my vision (straight lines appearing wavy to me). Nothing could be done about this. But the cloudiness in my vision was caused by the fluid that had leaked onto the macula. This could be cleared by the injections of Lucentis. Mr. O also told me that it was very unlikely that the condition of my eye

would deteriorate further. Once the fluid had been entirely re-
moved, the condition should remain stable. Further injections
would maintain that stability but would probably be needed
less often and might eventually become no longer necessary.

I had my third injection on June 7 and a fourth a month later.
At the time of the third injection, Mr. O showed me on the scan
how most of the fluid on the macula had disappeared, but there
was still some, on which the third injection might have some effect. I should stress that, as far as I understood it, there was no
inevitability about this. The injections could work more or less
well. By the time of the fourth injection, I had guessed, from ob-
serving the clarity of my vision, that all the liquid on the macula
had disappeared, and Mr. O showed me on the scan that this
was indeed the case. My eyesight was now as good as it would
get. Mr. O said that I could either have no more injections unless
something occurred or continue to have injections at lengthening
intervals. The latter seemed the safer option (I wonder whether
I would have been given that option at the eye clinic), and so
there would be a five-week interval before my next injection, a
six-week interval before the one after that, and so on.

A final word about the eye clinic at Addenbrooke's. When
I decided to have my third eye injection at the Spire Hospital, I had to cancel my appointment for that injection at Addenbrooke's. I telephoned the eye clinic, using the only phone
number available for contacting them. I got this message: "This
mailbox is full. Goodbye." I thought of people getting that message who were, as I had been recently, in considerable anxiety
about the deterioration of their eyesight. What would it be like
to hear those blunt words, "This mailbox is full. Goodbye"?

I have talked to quite a few people about their own experiences at the eye clinic, and they have been mixed. One man

related a story much like mine. Interestingly, his experience took place before the pandemic, suggesting that the problems are not merely the result of the recent pressures on the health service. But recently someone told me of a very different experience. He was going to have a cataract operation. After he had visited the clinic for a scan, he was phoned by a doctor who said they had detected in the scan the beginnings of macular degeneration in that eye. There was an issue about whether to proceed with the cataract operation at that point. So he was invited to a meeting at the clinic, where he was given tea and biscuits while no less than three doctors discussed with him the best way to proceed. I was quite staggered by this account. It is good to know that in some instances the clinic is treating patients with the attention and respect they deserve.

Elsewhere in the UK, there are much worse situations. The very morning I am writing this (August 24) I read the following in a letter in a newspaper from a reader in Milford Haven:

SIR—I have a visual impairment—macular degeneration—for which I should have injections at six-weekly intervals to protect my remaining sight. It is becoming increasingly difficult to get these appointments. . . .

It is nearly 10 weeks since my last injection. Following my most recent complaint, two weeks ago, I was told it could be a further two to four weeks before an appointment was available.

My complaint elicited a response from the health board, which accepted the "permanent impact on people's sight" and the effect that stress could have on patients' general health.

In spite of this, there is no sign to date of an appointment, so I go to bed each night wondering whether my sight will have deteriorated overnight.[2]

2. Pam Perceval-Maxwell, letter in *The Daily Telegraph*, August 24, 2022.

My heart goes out to this lady, who has had to go through that daily anxiety for much longer than I did.

When I first observed the totally unexpected improvement of my vision two days after the second injection, it seemed like waking from a bad dream. Another metaphor I used in my journal was the obvious one of coming out of a tunnel into the light. Another was that the clouds had been dispersed. I was no longer on a downward trajectory, but on a level plain. I felt like the psalmists when God set them in a broad place.[3] As far as I could tell at that stage, my eyesight seemed to have returned to the condition it was in just before the first injection, when I had the distorted vision (so alarming to me at that point) but not the cloudiness—or at least much less cloudiness. I observed that it was returning to the same, but that actually the same was now different because of the experience I had been through. Something regained is much more precious than something never lost.

In the following weeks I was again and again amazed by the increasing clarity of my vision. On June 4, just before the third injection, I wrote that I had been "taken aback by the improvement in the *clarity* of my left-eye vision in the last few days." That evening I realized I did not have to sit so close to the television. I could see the screen clearly, though with what I called "wonky" vision. Faces on the television were now clear, though somewhat distorted. In very good light, such as daylight or the light of my Serious Readers lamps, I could read reasonably well. I still found no difference between using my distance glasses and my reading glasses (this had been the case already toward the end of 2021). I would later find that once again I could read more easily by using my reading glasses. This was a

3. See Pss. 31:8; 118:5.

remarkable discovery because it suggested that the condition of my sight had returned to how it was some time in 2021.

On June 5, I wrote:

> *Through the window beside my armchair, I'm looking at the great sycamore tree, shining in the evening sun, rippling in the gentle wind. Thank you, Lord, that I can see it! Clearly!*

Such experiences of seeing things clearly again were so wonderful because I had thought they were never going to be possible. This restoration of my sight was not miraculous in any strict sense. It did not puzzle the medical people. It was the effect of the Lucentis. But it was nonetheless remarkable. My gratitude to God was no less—because his grace was at work through doctors and medical science. I felt favored entirely beyond expectation. From then onward, when people asked about my eyesight, I got into the habit of saying that it was restored way beyond my expectations.

In this chapter I have written about the consolation of knowing God's loving solidarity with me in a time of acute anxiety. But not all consolation is devotional. During the darkest period of my experience, I went back to my favorite among Tove Jansson's Moomin books. I read it on the Kindle (e-book reader) that I had recently purchased primarily to help me continue to read in bed before sleeping—a very well-entrenched habit that I would have found it hard to do without. The Kindle had two advantages: it enabled me to magnify the print, and it had its own illumination. So I could read with it whatever the quality of the light in the room. I was able to read with it not only in bed but also in the hospital during some of the periods of anxious waiting.

In difficult or unhappy times of their lives, people often turn to familiar books. I am told that these are often books first read in childhood. Maybe people associate such books with the uncomplicated happiness of childhoods untroubled by the anxieties of adult life. But in my case I did not read the Moomin books in childhood (they were not yet translated into English), though I did fall in love with the Moomins in the form of the strip cartoons. I must have first read the last of the books, *Moominvalley in November* (published in English in 1971),[4] in my late twenties. Although all the Moomin books possess adult as well as childhood appeal, this one is the most adult and, I would guess, not so easily appreciated by young children as the others. It would also be hard to appreciate if one had not read at least some of the earlier books. It is the Moomin book for Moomin addicts—like me!

This may seem paradoxical because the book is set in Moomin-valley, in and around the Moominhouse, at a time when the Moomin family (the central characters in the other Moomin books) is not there. More precisely, the family members are not physically there, but they are constantly evoked in the memories and imaginations of the characters who come to visit them. These characters have varied and often vague recollections of them.

The book is Tove Jansson's farewell to the Moomins. She said that after writing this book she could not return to the Moomins. In a sense she makes her last visit to Moominval-ley in the person of Toft, the orphan boy who, before ever going there, conjured Moominvalley in his imagination again and again with great accuracy, seeking in Moominmamma the mother he lacked. A hint is even given that Toft actually imag-ined Moominvalley into existence, just as, later in the story, he imagines a dangerous monster that gets out of his control.

4. Trans. Kingsley Hart (London: Ernest Benn, 1971).

Tove wrote the book after the death of her mother, who had been a model for the character of Moominmamma. In it she was returning to Moominvalley, but, like Toft, she does not find Moominmamma there. The novel leaves Toft about to meet her as the family returns to Moominvalley. Without this ending the book would be unbearably sad. We readers can reacquaint ourselves with the Moomins by going back to the earlier books, but for the author herself there could be no return of or to the family. She began instead to write adult novels.

The strongly felt absence of the Moomins gives the book an elegiac, sometimes wistful, tone, but it is not at all gloomy. The characters, some of whom are quite new in the Moomin books, are attractively and entertainingly depicted. Each of them has to come to terms with the inadequate impressions they have about the family they have in some way idolized, and each finds thereby a newly authentic way of being themselves.

Why did I find the book consoling? Perhaps in part because it took me off into an imaginary world with which I was very familiar. The book exudes a strong sense of place. The "happy valley" and the always hospitable Moominhouse are well known from the earlier books but nowhere so lovingly described. The absence of the Moomins themselves did not diminish my enjoyment of the book, because I have always loved the minor characters of Moominvalley. It is a special feature of the Moomin books that Tove herself, as talented a graphic artist as she was a writer, developed the illustrations along with the text. The two are interdependent. Since the characters are neither human nor recognizable animals, it would be hard to imagine them without seeing them. In this book the characters come to life through their visual as well as narrative appearance. They belong to an enchanted world that still enchants me.

11

The Colour of May

Three Poems with Commentary

THE COLOUR OF MAY (1)

(May 9, 2019)

My darling memories of May
are white: the hosts of cow parsley,
the flowing tresses of the queen
of May, the hawthorn, bridal white.
They are the crests of nature's waves.
They brighten every leafy lane
that leads to summer's wedding day.

Such innocence we have betrayed,
trampled and trodden down to build
our roads to nowhere. Spirit of dear life,
sprite of our springtide, Whitsun white,
defy death's brag and lift our eyes
to heed these luscious hints of heaven!
You are the summer that will never fade.

The Colour of May (2)

(May 9, 2022)

This May, eyes faltering, perilously
on edge, I feast them gluttonously on
the massed exuberance of cow parsley
along the edge of every path and field.

They swirl and swing beside me in the breeze,
leading me on to waving meadows where
a sea of billowing brightness drifts as far
as eyes like mine can see with fading ease.

Next year I may not get so strong a fix
or drink so heady a draught of Whitsun white,
and so I nudge my memory to snap
and hold this wonder in my inner sight.

The Colour of May (3)

(May 29, 2022)

Waist-deep in cow parsley I wade.
This is the parsley's year of grace.
With regal bounty, worthy of
its sobriquet, the Queen Anne's lace,
it lavishes its loveliness,
robe rather of the queen of heaven,
all virgin white and full of grace.

When plants were symbols God was here,
and daisies in the flowery mead
were each a mirror to his gaze.
Then friars would pray this path and trace
Christ's passion in the flowers that bleed.
That code has lost its power, but still
all nature's whiteness whispers, "Grace!"

These three poems were never intended to form a sequence until I wrote the third one. When I wrote the first, in the summer before the pandemic, I had no idea that three years later I would write the second. That it turned out to be three years to the very day is a completely undesigned coincidence that I did not notice until I sat down to write this chapter and looked up the dates when I wrote the poems. I love coincidences, maybe partly because of a lifetime of reading novels. I enjoy novels with plots, stories that go somewhere and reach unexpected but satisfying resolutions.[1] Often such plots turn on coincidences. (The oldest novel with a plot of this kind is the book of Esther in the Old Testament, a biblical book I have enjoyed since I was a teenager.) Plots that turn on coincidences are often condemned as unrealistic. Such coincidences do not happen in real life, nor are there often such satisfying resolutions. But in this respect I like novels to be better than real life. So when meaningful coincidences actually do happen (and even in real life I have the sense that they happen more often than should statistically be the case), I like the sense they give that my life is plotted. (The book of Esther is strangely exceptional among the books of the Bible in that it never refers explicitly to God. But its theological point is that God's providence is at work anonymously in the events of history. The coincidences on which its plot turns are means of drawing our

1. A good example, to give just one, is the novel I have just finished reading, Anthony Doerr's beautiful *All the Light We Cannot See* (London: Fourth Estate, 2015). Some early events in the story gain retrospective significance in light of unexpected and remarkable coincidences later in the story. The plotting is much too intricate for the outcomes to be in the least predictable, but as the story reaches its climax, the reader has the satisfying sense that all the pieces are coming together and fit. By contrast, I find the great Russian novels less than satisfying because their different strands of narrative meander without seeming to be going anywhere and do not contribute to a resolution that brings them all together.

attention to that. The book speaks to a world in which God does not appear or speak in the way that he seems to do in the Pentateuch. God may not appear in Esther, but he is in the plot!)

To a coincidence like the dates of the first two poems I do not attach great importance. If readers shrug their shoulders, muttering, "So what?" I will not be much concerned. But I like to think that such coincidences are little hints of God's grace. They make us consider whether God is more intimately involved in the plots of our lives than we generally suppose. Also, because they are so completely undesigned by us, they alert us to the much bigger ways in which our lives are not controlled by us. Things happen to us. What turns out is at least as much due to what happens to us as to what we deliberately do. We do not write the plot.

All three poems celebrate the "whiteness" of the month of May, with its hawthorn blossom and its cow parsley. The first and the second associate this with the fact that white recalls the name Whitsun (White Sunday, now usually called Pentecost), while the first and third reference the fact that white is also the symbol of virginity and therefore of bridal attire. The first poem may be the first poem about nature that I have written or at least the first that I considered successful. I didn't use to think I could write about nature. I have no expert knowledge of the natural world, although I have always had a strong feeling for it and could not imagine life unconnected from it. As the first poem also indicates, this is also, in part, the source of my horror at the destruction of nature in our time. In that poem May's whiteness is more of a memory than an observation, though it is a memory sparked by observation of what could still be seen of May's whiteness in the vicinity of my home. (In lines that didn't make their way into the poem, I spoke of the flowers "in these our urban sanctuaries of wild, caught, penned, and cosseted, to soothe our souls.") But that poem soon became the first of a series of poems on the twelve months of the year, all of which began from observation of features of nature in that month (and mostly celebrating the "colour" of that month). I have gone on to make nature poetry the kind I most often write, while these later poems have become more and more inspired by a sustained attention to particular creatures or ensembles of creatures.

The first poem, an unorthodox kind of sonnet, draws liberally on Shakespeare's eighteenth sonnet, probably the best known of his sonnets. These are the lines to which my poem alludes:

> Shall I compare thee to a summer's day? . . .
> Rough winds do shake the darling buds of May . . .
> But thy eternal summer shall not fade, . . .
> Nor shall death brag thou wander'st in his shade.[2]

I describe for its own sake what for Shakespeare is only an example of natural beauty ("the darling buds of May") with which to compare the man he addresses. Shakespeare's sonnet is not actually about nature; mine is. When I do, in the second stanza, address someone, it is the Holy Spirit, who came at Pentecost (Whitsun).

While Shakespeare laments the temporary nature of all earthly beauty ("every fair from fair sometime declines"), thinking only of his friend, I lament the damage we have done to nature, turning "leafy lanes" to "roads to nowhere." Shakespeare counteracts the certainty that his friend's beauty will

2. Quotations from the sonnet follow *The Oxford Book of Sonnets*, ed. John Fuller (Oxford: Oxford University Press, 2000), 38.

fade with the certainty that his sonnet will give it immortality. As long as there are people to read his words, "thy eternal summer shall not fade." A closing claim that the sonnet "gives life to thee" convinces within the magic of the poem, but on reflection it is somewhat empty, since all we learn about the man from the poem is that Shakespeare thinks him more beautiful than a summer's day. It is the beauty of the sonnet that lives.

In my poem I appeal to the Holy Spirit to give the life of the new creation to the natural beauty we have trodden down. I transfer to this Creator-Spirit Shakespeare's address to his friend: "You are the summer that will never fade." Hope that nature will be delivered from transience is based not on the power of the poem, as in Shakespeare's sonnet, but on the power of God. It is wholly typical of my nature poetry that reflections on the natural world lead to thoughts of God and not infrequently to the hope of a renewal of the whole creation when God takes his creation into his eternity.

In addition to its deliberately obvious debt to Shakespeare, the poem contains a more distant echo of one of the finest and best-known Christian poems about the natural world: Gerard Manley Hopkins's "God's Grandeur" (also a sonnet).[3] My words "trampled and trodden down" will remind many readers of Hopkins's line: "Generations have trod, have trod, have trod." My words (with the repeated "tr" sound and the repeated "d" sound) attempt the same effect as Hopkins's repeated "trod." They evoke a continued and thoughtlessly destructive subduing of nature's life. It is salutary to recall that Hopkins's poem was written in 1877, when most of the countryside of England and Wales (Hopkins wrote the poem at St. Beuno's in Wales) was much as it had been at least since the agricultural revolu-

3. *Oxford Book of Sonnets*, 227.

tion of the previous century. His reference to many "generations" must mean that he partly had farming practices in mind,
those that represented increasingly intensive human use of
the natural world with no regard for its beauty and integrity.
But he undoubtedly was thinking also, probably mainly, of
the foundries and factories of the Industrial Revolution. He
later described a location in the vicinity of Manchester as "a
darksome place, with pits and mills and foundries."[4] We now
deplore the destruction of the countryside by industrialized
farming, road building (as in my poem), and massive urban ex-
pansion. Hopkins's poem resonates with contemporary readers
probably even more than it did with readers in his own time.
Of course, the English countryside has been shaped by human
use over many centuries. What so many of us now deplore is
the change from what might be regarded as human collabora-
tion with the natural world to massive destruction of it. People
of my generation inevitably remember the countryside as it
was in our youth. Not much of that countryside remains, and
my poem reflects that, while "roads to nowhere" suggests the
pointlessness of much of what has replaced it. The relentless
pursuit of high-speed travel from everywhere to everywhere
else has destroyed much of what we used to think worth traveling to see.

In reaction to such destruction, both Hopkins's poem and
mine turn to the Holy Spirit, the Creator-Spirit who is the ultimate source of nature's vitality. Whether I was actually influenced by this aspect of Hopkins's poem I am not sure. The
thought of Whitsun (White Sunday, so called apparently because baptisms used to take place then and the baptized wore
white) suggested the Holy Spirit to me, but the way I refer to

4. Quoted in Norman H. Mackenzie, *A Reader's Guide to Gerard Manley Hopkins* (London: Thames & Hudson, 1981), 65.

the "Spirit of dear life" looks like a reminiscence of Hopkins's phrase "the dearest freshness," while my "sprite of our spring-tide" chimes with Hopkins's use of the word *springs* for the dawn that symbolizes the giving of new life to trampled nature by the Holy Spirit. Since I knew Hopkins's poem well, some such influence on my poem is likely, but the fact that I can't be sure about it is an indication that critics should not be too confident in identifying the sources of a poet's imagination.

Hopkins's last stanza expresses confidence that "nature is never spent," because the divine Spirit is the source of its life. Nature is certainly resilient, and if we humans were to disappear tomorrow from the United Kingdom, nature would very rapidly take over again. Chernobyl is a well-known example of biodiversity flourishing in a space abandoned by humans. But species we have driven to extinction cannot revive themselves, and new species take millennia to develop. In any case, we are not likely to disappear any time soon. It is difficult to be as confident now as Hopkins was. In pollution and climate change we see nature, in a sense, fighting back, but at our expense. The mutual impoverishment of humans and nature that Hopkins already detected is very far advanced. What of the endlessly creative power of the Holy Spirit, which Hopkins evokes so memorably in the last two lines of his sonnet? I do not doubt it, but my poem reckons with a perhaps more comprehensive re-creation of the natural world through participation in the eternal life of God, comparable with and accompanying the resurrection of dead humanity. The Creator-Spirit, who is the divine life itself, is "the summer that will never fade."

My second "Colour of May" poem is very different from the first. It has, as far as I know, no literary sources. It aims to convey much more directly my immediate impressions of nature and the feelings I had at the time. I began writing it in my head while experiencing what it describes and completed it within hours. It also reflects the fact that, since writing "The Colour of May (1)" three years previously, I had become more skilled at describing nature as I directly experienced it.

It was written just two days before my visit to the eye clinic at Addenbrooke's for the second injection. This was at the point in my story when my eyesight was at its worst. I was suffering from considerable anxiety, and it was in the hope of relieving it somewhat that I took a walk to the nearby village of Grantchester. Grantchester is about half an hour's walk from my home. I walked there along paths that run beside the road and then back by the alternative route, across Grantchester Meadows (the meadows mentioned in the second stanza). (Devotees of the TV version of James Runcie's Grantchester novels will be familiar with these meadows.) These walks are very familiar to me, but they were distinguished on this occasion by the exceptional abundance of cow parsley.

It was a fantastically good year for cow parsley, as everyone who noticed it agreed. In the third of these poems I call it "the parsley's year of grace" (using an old-fashioned way of saying "year of our Lord," or anno Domini). Along the paths and beside the fields on my outward journey, there were thick rows of cow parsley, and when I got to the meadows I was amazed at the huge mass of the parsley stretching from the path to the river. I had certainly never seen it like that before. The poem describes the cow parsley as I saw it, very conscious of the cloudiness of my vision. I remember from time to time I looked closely at the intricate beauty of the little flowerlets composing each spray of flowers, thinking that I might never see them properly again, just as I might never again be able to read. It was a particularly intense experience, as I hope the poem conveys. From the notes in which I composed the poem in stages, I see that it went through very few developments. There are hardly any words or phrases that did not get into the finished text. This is partly because I worked out much of it in my head while walking, but also because the words seemed to come quite easily. Not all my poems *feel* inspired, but this one did.

For several years I have emailed most of my poems, as soon as I have finished them, to a small number of friends who I know enjoy my poetry. Sometimes people respond with comments. Here are two responses I received to this poem:

> I thought this was a wonderful poem. . . . Very poignant of course, and moving. But also true for all of us in this fragile life.

> I have just read your poignant but beautiful poem about the cow parsley. I was very moved by it but also thought it was such a good poem too in the way it captured the movement of the flower heads and the joy of seeing them appear every year. . . . I was photographing the cow parsley near the cricket pavilion on Sunday morning. It is glorious and I wanted to capture the memory of it. Your poem has helped me to do that in a different, more visceral way.

I was glad to find that the poem had more than a private meaning. When people are moved by my poetry, I feel I must be doing something worthwhile.

The third "Colour of May" poem was finished toward the end of the month. Conscious now of completing a series of three, I deliberately adopted the same idiosyncratic sonnet form as I had used for the first of the poems, though the rhyme "scheme" varies. (I say "scheme" because it is less a scheme than an irregular means of getting the word *grace* to echo through the poem.)

I used to think cow parsley is so called because cows eat it. I guess many people think that. But according to Richard Mabey, it "simply means (in reference to the leaves) an inferior version of real parsley."[5] Of course, that does not settle the question whether cows actually eat cow parsley. On a later visit to Grantchester Meadows, I saw a herd of about a dozen cows wandering through the great sea of cow parsley. Unfortunately, I wasn't able to see if they were actually eating it. But I assume that's why they were there. They looked happy. From the internet I learned that horses, sheep, and goats all love cow parsley, and I even found a photo of a cow looking eagerly at a spray of it.

It is also known as Queen Anne's lace, though Mabey says that this name "has never become widely used, despite no end of elaborate stories to explain its origin as a name." According to one account that he quotes, Queen Anne suffered from asthma and used to walk in the countryside because of its fresher air. As she and her ladies walked the country lanes, they carried their lace pillows and made lace. The lacy flowers of the cow parsley resembled the patterns of the ladies' lace, and so the country people started to call it Queen Anne's lace. Mabey is skeptical of this and other such stories and, disappointingly, thinks it more likely that the name comes from North America.[6] But he does not explain why the Americans should have called it that.

My poem also alludes to Queen Anne's Bounty, an Act of Parliament that gave support to the poorer clergy of the Church of England, but the allusion merely serves to evoke the ideal of the lavish generosity appropriate to a queen.[7] In its fabulous

5. Richard Mabey, *Flora Britannica* (London: Chatto & Windus, 1996), 283.
6. Mabey, *Flora Britannica*, 283.
7. The image of a queen is also picked up from the first of these poems, where "the flowing tresses of the queen of May" are the hawthorn (or may) blossoms.

"year of grace," the cow parsley "lavishes its loveliness" on all of us. But rather than the image of an English queen's lacy attire, a more appropriate image of its exceptional loveliness would be the robe of the Virgin Mary, known in Catholic tradition as the Queen of Heaven.[8] Though the robe of the Virgin is usually depicted as blue, white would also suit her, since it is the color symbolic of virginity.

The second stanza was inspired by the Franciscan Gardens in Canterbury. I took a short holiday in Canterbury in late May, when my eyesight had begun to improve. The Franciscans had a friary in Canterbury in the medieval period until it was dissolved by Henry VIII. Not much of the buildings survives, but there is now an ongoing project to restore the gardens to how they might have been in the time of the Franciscans. I visited the gardens on a sunny day and enjoyed their peace as well as their beauty. In the medieval period a "flowery mead" was a lawn studded with tiny flowers. The friars gave plants religious significance as symbols of the key elements of the Christian faith. Periwinkles symbolized the death of Jesus and snowdrops his resurrection. For us twenty-first-century people, it is hardly possible to believe that the natural world has this kind of symbolism encoded in it by its Creator. But approaching nature with Christian faith, as I do in my nature poetry, we can let the natural world remind us of its Creator and his attributes and the way in which he has redeemed us in Christ. Here in this poem I suggest that nature "whispers." It may no longer proclaim God with a voice that everyone hears loud and clear, but to those of us who know its Creator, it reminds us of him, and even to those who do not, its abundance of beauty may still whisper, "All this has been freely and generously *given* to us. We did not make it. Must there not be a Giver, *someone* to whom we can give thanks?"

8. My use of this title is imaginative, not theological.

The word *grace* appears at the end of both stanzas, picking up its use at the end of the second line. It is emphasized also by the rhymes ("lace," "trace"). It is the key word of the poem. For many people it is a word that requires explanation, because its use in English versions of the New Testament and in Christian prayer and discourse has little connection with the way the word is otherwise mostly used (referring to elegance or beauty of form or movement). The Greek word usually translated "grace" is *charis*. It is one of those Greek words that were rather unremarkable in their ordinary use but that early Christians made into ways of saying some very distinctively Christian things. (Another word of that sort is the Greek word *agapē*, which is the usual word in the New Testament for "love.")

Charis means basically "giving"—not so much "gift," in the sense of the thing that is given, but "giving," in the sense of the act of giving. In 2 Corinthians 8:9, for example, Paul uses it to mean God's act of generous self-giving to us that is the story of Jesus. In the New International Version, the translation is, "You know the grace of our Lord Jesus Christ, that though he was rich, yet for your sake he became poor, so that you through his poverty might become rich." Other translations put "grace" into modern English in different ways. The Revised English Bible has, "You know the generosity of our Lord Jesus Christ: he was rich, yet for your sake he became poor." But that isn't quite adequate. The sentence does describe generosity. The Lord impoverished himself. He gave away all his wealth to make us rich. But grace is not a quality of God, an attitude, or a disposition. It's what God does. It's his act of generous giving. So the New Revised Standard Version has perhaps the best rendering: "You know the generous act of our Lord Jesus Christ, that though he was rich, yet for your sakes he became poor." Grace is that act of giving for others. It is not just God's attitude toward us, and it is certainly not, as people sometimes imagine, some kind of stuff that God doles out to us. It is God's generosity in action, and its extraordinary climax is God's giving of himself for us in Jesus Christ. It is Jesus's life of utter self-giving for others, Jesus's giving up his life so that we may live. Grace is God's love in self-sacrificing action for us.

In the poem I use the traditional phrase "full of grace" for the Virgin Mary. It is based on the angel's words to Mary in Luke 1:30, but the sense of the Greek is much better conveyed by the modern translations, which mostly agree in rendering: "you have found favor with God."[9] God's grace to Mary is his generous act of choosing her to be the mother of Jesus. She is, as a modern Christmas carol puts it, the "most highly favored lady." Grace is not something she has but God's act of remarkable giving to her.

Creation is God's gift, not just in the beginning but endlessly as God gives and sustains the life of all creatures in their incalculable number and diversity. Creation is God's continuous act of abundantly generous giving to all his creatures. Like salvation, creation is grace.

In every true act of giving, a giver gives their love as well as the gift. To receive a gift as a gift from its giver is to receive far more than the gift itself. It is to recognize and receive the giver's love. So it is with God and creation. "All nature's whiteness whispers, 'Grace!'"

Looking at the three poems now, I see how different the second is from the others. The first and third poems are re-

9. For example, this translation is found not only in the (Protestant) NIV but also in the (Catholic) RNJB. The phrase "full of grace" is an English translation of the Vulgate Latin version.

flective. They see meaning in the white blossoms of May by relating them to wider reflections on nature and God. Though both begin with a reference to myself, there is no first-person language in the rest of them. The second poem, by contrast, is entirely personal. It simply expresses with some intensity how I perceived and felt about the cow parsley during one walk at a point of crisis in my life. In that context my vision narrowed to just me and the cow parsley.

> When angels robed in white
> take holidays from heaven,
> I wonder if they might
> wander with cows in fields
> of cow parsley so bright
> even their shining eyes
> must boggle at the sight.
> They marvel at its grace.
> Each makes a chain to wear
> around his golden hair.
> They call it angels' lace.
> So when they soar in flight
> back to the holy place,
> the humble cow parsley,
> bathed in celestial light,
> bows to the throne of grace.

12

Christ in Three Sightings
A Poem with Commentary

Perfect and patient Master of the way,
teach me again the lessons of my past:
that in my weakness I will find your power,
that losing is the only way to find,
that every seed must fall before it flower.

Faithful and fond Companion on the way,
carry the burdens that I cannot bear.
The path is steep, steeper than I could guess
when you invited me to walk with you.
But this is not a choice I can escape.
I scramble upward under your duress.

Dauntless and mighty Master of the deep,
alone you quell its enmity.
I foundered and I fell far down.
I clasped and clung to you. Your arm
was strong to save. You set me on
a shore already known to me,

but now with sunlit clarity
the contours of your love I see.

The first two stanzas of this poem were written at the most difficult time in the story I have told: around the time of my second eye injection. The third stanza was written later, in Sandwich, Kent, during the short holiday I took in Canterbury near the end of May.

In the first stanza the "lessons of my past" are those I have learned in both knowledge and experience. They are characterized by the three scriptural allusions in lines 3–5. First, there is the theme of God's power in human weakness, which is one of the dominant themes of Paul's Second Letter to the Corinthians. This has long been my favorite Pauline letter, and I wrote about this theme in 2 Corinthians in an essay (based on a sermon) published forty years ago.[1] Since then this theme has again and again been a feature of my life with God in both major and minor experiences, including now the crisis about my eyesight.

Fundamental to the way Paul understands his experience in 2 Corinthians is that he shares in the ordinary frailty and vulnerability, both physical and psychological, that belongs to the human condition in this world. Neither his status as a Christian nor his calling as an apostle means that God turns him into some kind of superman. The power of God is at work in his life and ministry, but characteristically in the context of his weak and vulnerable humanity (see 2 Cor. 4:7; 12:8–10). In pursuit

---

1. Richard Bauckham, "Weakness—Paul's and Ours," *Themelios* 7, no. 3 (1982): 4–6. This article can be accessed at https://biblicalstudies.org.uk /article_weakness_bauckham.html.

of his apostolic calling, Paul was constantly pushing himself to the limits of his own resources. He experienced all sorts of troubles, including at least one experience of only narrowly escaping death. In these circumstances Paul learned to trust in God, not in his own abilities. The power of God at work in his life and circumstances is evident in the way he reaches the limits of his endurance, but these experiences of suffering do not overwhelm or overcome him:

> We are afflicted in every way, but not crushed;
> perplexed, but not driven to despair;
> persecuted, but not forsaken;
> struck down, but not destroyed. (2 Cor. 4:8–9 [NRSV modified])

The Corinthians were inclined to think that Paul's weakness threw doubt on his claim to be an apostle. But for Paul, his very evident human weakness made it clear that the power of the gospel at work through his ministry was the power of God, not his own achievement (4:7).

In these experiences Paul's life was conformed to his gospel of the crucified and risen Jesus. For Jesus himself shared in all the frailty and vulnerability of human life to the extent of suffering a humiliating and excruciatingly painful death. The power of God did not exempt him from suffering but took effect through the weakness of the cross when God raised him from death (see 1 Cor. 1:25). So for Paul, it was the dying of Jesus that he experienced in his own frailty and sufferings (2 Cor. 1:5; 4:10–11), and it was the power of Jesus's resurrection that he experienced in every escape from death, every encouragement received after anxiety and depression, every convert made in the midst of persecution, every consolation given in seeming failure (1:3–7; 4:7–12; 7:5–7).

As humans, and even as Christians, we are prone to rely on our own abilities as though they were absolutely our own rather than given and sustained by God. We may need those common experiences in which we reach the limits of our abilities and find that we cannot cope in order to realize that our abilities are limited. Such experiences bring home to us the need to trust in God. It is God who enables us to keep going when life gets really hard. It is God who enables us to complete the task that seems too much for us. It is God who rescues us from despair. It is God who consoles us when we feel forsaken. It is God who steps in to save us from the temptations that are too much for us to resist. It is God who gives us the help of family, friends, medical professionals, counselors, and others when we cannot help ourselves.

Of course, God is also at work in our strengths and our successes, but it is easy to ignore that. When we know that we are weak, we know that we must rely on God. I have found again and again that at the limits of my coping there is God. This is especially true, as it was for Paul, in the service of God. Anyone who knows only their strength and not their weakness cannot have given themselves to a task that demands all they can give. But discovering the power of God in our weakness is an invaluable experience. We learn to find in our weakness the compassionate solidarity of the crucified Christ. In that form of divine love we also have the assurance that, by God's grace, we will pull through. We may not recover our health or achieve what had proved too much for us, but we will not be overwhelmed or overcome by these experiences. In some way we will experience already in our weakness the power of God that raised Jesus, sustaining our faith and our love. The power that will raise us, with Jesus, from death already makes a difference in the weakness of our mortal lives.

The second scriptural allusion ("losing is the only way to find") points to a saying of Jesus that occurs, remarkably, six times in the four Gospels:[2]

> Whoever seeks to gain their life will lose it,
> but whoever loses their life will keep it. (Luke 17:33, my
> translation)[3]

This is the basic version of the saying. In its other occurrences, phrases are added that make clear its meaning. In most cases, "whoever loses their life" is expanded with "for my sake" or "for my sake, and for the sake of the gospel" (Matt. 10:39; 16:25; Mark 8:35; Luke 9:24), making clear that the kind of losing life that is envisaged is not mere recklessness, but self-sacrifice out of devotion to the cause of Christ. In John 12:25, there are major variations, but the substance and structure of the aphorism are the same.

The saying is one of those compact aphorisms of Jesus that work by challenging us to understand the paradox they present. The different contexts in which this saying occurs in the Gospels show that it was seen to be relevant to Christian life in more ways than one. In several cases martyrdom, the ultimate way of giving one's life for Christ, following his own example, is clearly in view. But in other cases, especially Luke 9:24 (following the use of "daily" in 9:23), a broader application to the renunciation of self throughout a life of discipleship is envisaged.

2. Matt. 10:39; 16:25; Mark 8:35; Luke 9:24; 17:33; John 12:25.
3. I use "their" as a common gender singular possessive pronoun, a practice that is now widely accepted. Some modern translations (such as the NRSV) avoid "his" by making the subject plural ("those who"), but biblical aphorisms of this kind regularly refer to the individual, not the group. This is deliberate and should be reflected in the translation.

This is easier to understand if we realize that the term *psychē*, translated "life," strongly approaches the meaning "self." The paradox of the saying challenges us to consider what is *true* life or the *real* self. Is it the selfish, self-aggrandizing self that clings to its life or the selfless, self-giving self that gives itself away?

The attempt to secure one's life by living it for one's own benefit is bound to fail because death comes to everyone and is the end of what the selfish person is trying to keep. To live one's life as though one owns it and can use it and keep it for oneself is an illusion that death will always destroy. But there is also a sense in which living for oneself destroys life already before death. In grasping and hoarding their life for their own pleasure, the selfish person finds that the real fulfillment they seek escapes them even before life itself escapes them in death. The true self cannot be found that way.

The person, on the other hand, who renounces the path of self-gratification and expends their life in self-giving for God and for others finds their life given back to them by God. They keep their life by losing it. One could say that they lose the false self and find the true self, the self they are given by God and receive from God in place of the illusory self that attempts to live independently of God. In every act of self-giving, a blow is dealt to the old, self-aggrandizing self, and the new self gains ground. If this is true, then the supreme act of self-giving, martyrdom, must be the most complete instance of the saying's truth. The one who gives their life in death will receive it again in eternal life. The old self is definitively renounced and the new self given.

In John 12:25 the saying is found in a unique context, in which Jesus applies it to himself, with reference to his death and resurrection. Here it follows a saying unique to John's Gospel: "Unless a grain of wheat falls into the earth and dies, it remains just a single grain; but if it dies, it bears much fruit" (12:24).

This saying accounts for the third allusion in the first stanza of my poem: "every seed must fall before it flower." Although Jesus says this with reference to his own death and resurrection, it is also clear from the context (see 12:26) that his way of the cross is the pattern for his disciples to follow, not only by martyrdom if required but also before death in their lives of discipleship. Jesus's death is not only something he does for us but also something reflected in the shape of Christian living. The old self must continually die, "crucified" with Christ, as Paul puts it (Rom. 6:6; Gal. 2:20), so that the new self may share in the life of his resurrection.

When I wrote the lines "that losing is the only way to find, / that every seed must fall before it flower," I had in mind, of course, the deterioration in my eyesight. I was reckoning with the possibility of losing my ability to read or, at best, of being able to read only with considerable effort. This was not a matter of voluntary renunciation or sacrifice. I had no choice in the deterioration of my eyesight. But I did accept that loss as God's will for me. In what sense I would "find" or "flower," I don't think I had any idea. I merely had the conviction that, according to those sayings of Jesus, some kind of new flowering of my life with God must be God's intention for me. It need not look like flowering from any other perspective, but from the perspective of knowing God and following Jesus, it would be so.

These were "lessons of my past" that in writing this stanza of the poem I was asking Jesus the Teacher to teach me again. (By "Master of the way," I meant the one who had himself mastered the true way to life and taught it to others.) I had certainly reflected quite deeply on those sayings of Jesus, especially the paradoxical aphorism about losing life and finding it.[4] But I meant also that I had learned them in experience. In all human lives, loss happens in many guises. For me the big losses, the ones that were hard to cope with, were not, I have to admit, heroic acts of self-sacrifice. They happened to me. In such experiences it is not easy to discern and accept God's will in them. But in the long run I learned to do so and that life with God is as full of "finds" as it is of losses. It is a matter of recognizing the pattern of Jesus's cross and resurrection working through one's life.

Sometimes we can lose something very precious to us and actually have that very thing restored to us. I recall an example that a colleague of mine in the theology faculty at the University of Manchester related to me long ago. Barnabas Lindars, in addition to being a professor in the faculty, was also an Anglican Franciscan. He told me how, when he realized he had a vocation to join the Franciscans, he had to renounce his plans for an academic career, for which he was very well qualified. Only some time later the Franciscans decided it would be good to have someone within the order in academic theology and asked Barnabas to pursue his academic research and to apply for a post at the University of Cambridge. What he had given up was given back to him, now as an integral part of his vocation from God in the Franciscan order. Something given up and then restored is the same but not just the same. It is experienced and valued differently. It is experienced as God's gift in a more profound way.

The paradigm case in the Bible is the story of Abraham's "sacrifice" of his son Isaac in Genesis 22. It is an endlessly fruitful story. Abraham is asked by God to give up his only and beloved son, who was not only dear to him but also the one

---

4. For example, see my essay "The Christian Way of Losing and Finding Self," in Richard Bauckham, *The Bible in the Contemporary World* (London: SPCK; Grand Rapids: Eerdmans, 2016), 138–43.

through whom God's wonderful promises to Abraham were to be fulfilled. The son God had given him, the heir essential to the promises God had given him—all this Abraham was to renounce for God's sake. The test was to determine whether Abraham's devotion to God really took precedence over everything else in his life. But when he passes the test, everything is given back to him. Isaac does not die. A key point for appreciating the significance of the story is that Isaac is now doubly given—given by God when he was conceived, given back to Abraham on the mountain—and doubly precious. In Abraham's experience, what happened was virtually a giving of his son up to death and a receiving of him back restored to life.

What was required of Abraham was extreme, and that is why it can serve as a paradigm, with which we can align many lesser forms of sacrifice and surrender that may be required of us.[5] What I did not expect when I wrote the first stanza of the poem was that my ability to read, surrendered in principle to God, should he require it, would turn out to be something restored to me beyond expectation. The danger of losing it was never as great as I feared, and the sight in my left eye did not fully recover. But it changed forever the way I experience and value my eyesight. Had I thought about it, I must always have known that sight is a remarkable faculty, given to us by God, and so is specifically the ability to read, which had been of incalculable value in my own life. But I hadn't really thought about it. I have worn spectacles, because of my short sight, from a very early age, but that has not really made me consider how eyesight is both wonderful and fragile, dependent on the intricate but delicate mechanism of the eye. Losing central vision in my right eye made me glad to be able to rely on my left

5. Note also the extreme demands Jesus made on his disciples and the promise that what will be given is much more than what has been renounced: Mark 10:29–30.

eye, but for that reason it did not shake my world and leave me
trembling, as the prospect of losing central vision also in my
left eye did. After the intensity of that experience, the eyesight I
have is precious beyond words, and I cannot forget that I have
it as the gift of God's love.

———————————

The first stanza of this poem related a "sighting" of Jesus
Christ as the Teacher of the way; the second stanza relates a
"sighting" of him as the Companion on the way. It requires less
commentary than the first. I am reflecting on the journey of
discipleship, but with my specific vocation particularly in view,
since it was my vocation that was coming to seem much more
difficult in the days around my second eye injection.

The invitation to which this stanza refers was not a one-time
event in my early life but refers rather to the way in which, during my teenage years, I came to take very seriously the call of
the Christian to live in a way wholly orientated to God, seeking
to love God above all things. The image of the Christian life as
a journey in which we are accompanied by Jesus is not found
explicitly in the New Testament, but is often seen as evoked by
Luke's story of the disciples on the way to Emmaus, on which
they are joined in their journey by the risen Christ. However,
they do not recognize him, whereas in my use of the motif here
he is very much a recognized presence with me in my life. The
image might also recall the book of Tobit, with which this book
began. There have been many artistic representations of Tobias
accompanied on his journey by the archangel Raphael, no doubt
because Raphael was seen in this case as a type of Christ. But
again, the companion goes unrecognized until the journey's end,
when Raphael reveals that he is an angel sent by God. My use
of the image of Jesus as a companion on the way may well owe
something to the work of Shusaku Endo, the Japanese Catholic

novelist, who understood Jesus as the "eternal companion," the one who had to experience in his life and death all the pain and sorrows humans go through in order to become their eternal companion, actualizing God's love for them by accompanying them in love. For Endo, who had difficulty adapting to Western theology, this was an authentically Japanese way of knowing Christ.[6] Yet it is an image that feels very natural to me, and I think many Christians will recognize it as true to at least one aspect of their relationship with God in Christ.

The stanza focuses on the experience of facing unusual difficulty on the way, as it becomes steep. It is important that Jesus as companion do more than accompany. He must share the load to make it possible for me to continue. I did not entertain the possibility of discontinuing the journey, not because I was subject to some divine compulsion but because I had committed myself irrevocably to the way of discipleship. Jesus's "duress" means his insistence that following the way entails this uphill struggle. There is no easy way around it available.

This stanza has no scriptural allusions. But now I realize there are some resemblances to John Bunyan's account of Christian's ascent of the Hill Difficulty in *The Pilgrim's Progress*. It is more than twenty years since I last read the book, but maybe some unconscious memory of it was at work when I wrote the poem. In any case, it provides an interesting text for comparison with mine, although it lacks the theme of Jesus as companion on the way that is a key element in my stanza. Here are the relevant parts of Bunyan's narrative:

> I believe then, that they all went on till they came to the foot of an Hill, at the bottom of which was a Spring. There was also

6. See Emi Mase-Hasegawa, *Christ in Japanese Culture: Theological Themes in Shusaku Endo's Literary Works*, Brill's Japanese Studies Library 28 (Leiden: Brill, 2008), 117–19.

in the same place two other ways besides that which came straight from the Gate; one turned to the left hand, and the other to the right, at the bottom of the Hill: but the narrow way lay right up the Hill, (and the name of the going up the side of the Hill, is called *Difficulty*.) *Christian* now went to the Spring and drank thereof to refresh himself, and then began to go up the Hill; saying,

> This Hill, though high, I covet to ascend,
> The difficulty will not me offend:
> For I perceive the way to life lies here;
> Come, pluck up, Heart; lets neither faint nor fear:
> Better, tho difficult, th' right way to go,
> Then wrong, though easie, where the end is wo.

The other two also came to the foot of the Hill. But when they saw that the Hill was steep and high, and that there was two other ways to go . . . they were resolved to go in those ways. . . .

I looked then after *Christian*, to see him go up the Hill, where I perceived he fell from running to going, and from going to clambering upon his hands and his knees, because of the steepness of the place.[7]

Christian's song reminds me of the vigorous faith that I recognized in "St. Patrick's Breastplate" and that I believe I was given to see me through the crisis.

———————————

The third stanza was written later, after my eyesight had significantly recovered and during a short holiday I took, based in Canterbury. It was on a visit to the lovely medieval town of Sandwich, one of the old Cinque Ports, that I composed this

7. John Bunyan, *The Pilgrim's Progress*, ed. N. H. Keeble, Oxford World's Classics (Oxford: Oxford University Press, 1984), 34–35.

stanza. I was sitting, I remember, in bright sunshine outside a hotel where I had some lunch. The sunshine appears in the penultimate line of the stanza.

The stanza takes up images of peril and deliverance that are frequent in the Psalms, where deep waters often represent dangerous or even evil forces that threaten the psalmist. The psalmist is being overwhelmed by or sinking in these waters until the Lord draws him out and sets him on firm ground.[8] I did not have a particular psalm in mind, and I did not have the Psalms available to me when I wrote the stanza. So I was reimagining this imagery while conscious of its strong background in the Psalms and of the fact that these psalmists praise and thank the Lord for their deliverance from extreme dangers.

The image of God stilling the sea, in the second line of the stanza, has distinctive sources (Pss. 89:9; 107:25–30). In the Hebrew Bible, only God has the power to control the raging sea (Job 38:8–11; Pss. 89:8–9; 104:6–9). But in my poem, the "Master of the deep" is Jesus Christ, and so I am also alluding to the miracle of the stilling of the storm in the Gospels (Mark 4:35–41), where the disciples' question "Who then is this, that even the wind and the sea obey him?" (4:41) has the implication that Jesus must be divine.

The sentence "Your arm was strong to save" came to me as though it were a reminiscence of the Psalms, and it does have a quite close parallel there (Ps. 77:15). But I think a more influential source was the hymn that begins "Eternal Father, strong to save / Whose arm hath bound the restless wave." It is the well-known hymn "for those in peril on the sea," which itself alludes both to God the Father's control over "the mighty ocean deep" and to Christ's calming of the waters.

8. See Pss. 18:16; 40:2; 69:1–2, 14–15; 118:5; 124:4–5; also Jon. 2:2–6. In Ps. 107:25–30, the description of a dangerous storm at sea is literal.

In the last four lines I develop in my own way the idea that God delivers from the perils of the sea and sets one on firm ground. My thought here is that, after such an experience, the same is no longer the same. Life after deliverance by God is life received from God as the gift of his love. However well one might have known all along that everything is God's gift, now this is an inescapable and joyful recognition. The place to which God restores one now features the contours of God's love, seen "with sunlit clarity." That phrase was given to me by the fact that I wrote the stanza sitting in bright sunlight, but it was also prophetic. Although I was glad of the extent to which I could now see well, it would be later that I was struck by the greater clarity that resulted from the fuller effects of the eye injections.

13

Three Poems on Sight

WOODLAND SIGHT

Today the world feels kind
and consolation comes
like song and sun
filtering through the shade
of this untroubled glade.

Among these undulating boughs
that swoop like birds of prey
across my way, I find my sight
rhymes with the naturalness of woods
and lakes where plants that float
in flat curvaceous shapes
uplift their blossoms, white
as mountain peaks
that brighten into sight.

*Note: The second stanza alludes to the distortion in my eyesight.
I now see straight lines as wavy lines, like the "undulating boughs."*

"My Eyes Have Seen Your Salvation" (Luke 2:30)

So long he lived for this.
Death stalked his days,
impatient to be seen,
trying to catch his eye
as he stumbled peering in the dusk.

The temple was the place.
Here glory sometimes peeked
out of the great clouds of smoke
like Sinai. At night there were torches
and songs of yearning hope.

Now it was through no dimness that he saw
his and all hearts' desire,
and parents he must tell
that for the joy of all the world
they must forfeit their own.

He gazed until he felt his sight reborn.
His words welled from a spring of ancient meaning
newly unstopped.
His wonderment will wing
like some huge legendary bird
into eternity.

"Now I See" (John 9:25)

Into my dimness light splashed.
I was dumbfounded.
Who can name this surging brilliance?

Now with eyes redeemed,
washed full of sight,
I see the light
streaming, free-flowing,

wild and profusely
from the fount of grace.

I see
a luminous world
of meadow flowers
and rippling trees,
birds tumbling out of sunlight,
glistening drops
from summer showers.

In pools of light,
the looking-glasses of the sky,
I see
reflected glory,
earth's returning praise,
all the bright brimmingness
of daylit hours.

At last I see
the haloed head,
the rainbow coloured light
of this new freshened world,
who mixed the mud
and spat the sight into my eyes.
I worshipped.
Who can name this radiance?
Who can doubt his all-redeeming powers?

*Note: In this poem I am imagining the experience of the man who
had been blind from birth and was healed by Jesus. Of course, my
own experience was quite different, but it helped me appreciate
just how wonderful sight is. The poem tries to express this by
imagining the experience of this man who had never known sight
until Jesus gave it to him.*

14

Brown Grass

A Poem

As these tall grasses sway,
wind-tossed and tawny,
back and then bowing,
tumbling and rising,
so my life, shaken,
blown and suspiring,
lurching, it seems, and lifted,
feels, as it riffles through me,
unseen the hand of God.

Then for one exquisite moment
they slow,
paused by the stillness,
fragile seed-heads
balanced in the shining air.
I too breathe this ripe moment,
no longer rocked but gently
held in the unseen arms,
seeking love's face.

15

Thanksgiving

Somehow nothing has happened I feel,
Nothing mine and nothing for real,
Till I seal it with outbursts of thanks.
—Micheal O'Siadhail, *Testament*[1]

The upshot of the story I have told in this book must be thanksgiving. In the period immediately after the partial recovery of my sight, when I saw that my fears of losing the ability to read were not going to be realized, my gratitude to God was intense. The whole experience had been intense. I lived through a crisis in my life. The intensity of such an experience is bound to wane. But intense experiences leave their mark on us. After them life may seem to return to normal, but we are not the same. Such experiences can be defining moments in our life stories, experiences to which we often look back and

1. Micheal O'Siadhail, *Testament* (Waco: Baylor University Press, 2022), 26. These lines are from "psalm" 23 in O'Siadhail's "Psalter."

from which we get our bearings for living. Something about the experiences imparts a new quality or character to the life we continue to live. Not everything that seems important at the time remains so in hindsight, but defining moments do. I think the fact that I lived through this experience very consciously with God accounts for my sense that my thankfulness to God in this instance is not merely the conclusion to an episode of my life that is now past. It feels as though the experience has made gratitude to God a more pervasive feature of my life from now on. I do not mean that thanksgiving has not been important in my life with God before now. Of course it has. But it feels as though thanksgiving has, as it were, risen up higher in the scale of my attitudes to God and life.

Unsurprisingly, there have been times when I have caught myself thinking that actually life is now just the same as it was before this story began. This seems to me analogous to the way many of us experienced emerging from the pandemic. After those two very strange years of lockdowns, restrictions, and the deprivation of many aspects of our lives as they used to be, it was natural to feel relief that everything was returning to normal. We busied ourselves reverting to how we used to live. But we also knew very well that we were not the same. Those two years must have had permanent effects, for good or ill, on how we understand ourselves and the world. We may not be able to identify those effects at all accurately. They may become apparent only in more distant retrospect. But effects, different for different people, there undoubtedly have been.

Similarly, I know that only in a superficial sense have I returned to the "normal" of life before the sight in my left eye deteriorated. Anything precious that is lost and restored is no longer the same. It is better, because after loss we become more appreciative of its value. Something we may have taken for granted can no longer be taken for granted. We are newly and gladly aware that it is, and has always been, gift. And true gifts always come with the love that inspired the giver. If we have come to take the giver's love for granted, restoration comes with a renewed and intensified sense of that love. Gratitude is in the end always gratitude for someone's love.

It would, I imagine, be possible for me to pretend to myself that nothing has changed and to suppress the continuing gratitude to God that would otherwise color my life. But something about this experience, by the grace of God, makes that more difficult to do. My sight has been only partially restored. Most notably, the distortion that makes me see straight lines as wavy remains and is permanent. I have got used to it. In some situations, such as writing with a pen or typing onscreen, the distortion gets my conscious attention more than in others. This means I cannot forget that my eyesight is now different. And so, paradoxically, a respect in which my sight has not been restored to what used to seem normal is a permanent reminder that I did go through an experience of loss and partial recovery of sight. It reminds me that sight is very precious, that it should never be taken for granted, and that I can thank God for the eyesight I have, impaired though it is.

I am tempted to compare the distortion in my eyesight with Jacob's limp. In the mysterious story of Jacob's nocturnal struggle with an angel (or was it God himself?), Jacob prevails and obtains a blessing, but he is also wounded in the hip (Gen. 32:24–31). Paradoxically, Jacob's limp becomes a sign and reminder of the blessing he received.

Psychological research has shown that gratitude is good for our mental health. (It boosts positive brain chemicals and inhibits those that cause stress.) Advice on healthy lifestyles now recommends we spend a few minutes each day focusing on the good things that have happened to us. ("Count your blessings," we used to say.) No doubt this is beneficial, but it falls far short of real gratitude or thanksgiving. Gratitude is being grateful *to someone*. Thanksgiving means giving thanks *to someone*. Thanking "life" or "our lucky stars" or "the universe" makes little sense because these entities have no intentionality. They do not care whether we are happy or miserable, flourish or flounder. When we receive a gift from someone, we think of that person and feel happy that they felt for us whatever form of goodwill prompted the gift. That is gratitude. Then we may actually tell them that we are grateful. That is thanksgiving. A gift is especially meaningful if it is from someone who loves us. Then it conveys not just itself but also the other person's love. We can treasure even small token gifts when we know that they come with love. Thanksgiving in this case is a way of completing the act of love. The gift and the thanks together create or enhance a bond of love between the giver and the recipient.

The story of Jesus's healing of the ten lepers is instructive (Luke 17:11–19). The healing takes place as they are on their way to the priest, who can certify their freedom from the disease. Jesus tells them to do this. Nine of them, when they find they have been healed, simply continue on their way to the priest. But one of the ten returns, praising God, to express his thanks to Jesus. It is to this man that Jesus says, "Your faith has made you well" (17:19). All the lepers had been healed, but the one who gave thanks was made whole in a fuller sense. It is not just that he owed Jesus his thanks and did right to express it. More than that, his experience of the healing was enhanced by his praise of God and thanks to Jesus. He completed, as it were, the circle of love that began with his healing by Jesus and returned to its source when he gave thanks. The gift is experienced as love and creates a bond of love when thanks is given.

The importance not merely of feeling gratitude but of actually expressing thanks to the giver of a gift can be seen when people benefit from something generous done for them by a stranger, such as the donation of a bodily organ or help given by a passerby who then goes on their way. Often people want to find out who the donor or helper was so that they can thank them. In special cases, such as saving a life, a bond of friendship may be created.

When we look back over our lives or even over the events of a single day and take note of all the good things, we see there is much for which we can be grateful to specific people, but there is also much for which there is no one but God to thank. Appreciating all those blessings but having no intentional Source to thank for them is one of the impoverishments of unbelief. Gratitude cannot truly be itself when it has no recipient. But the impoverishment begins in the receipt of the blessings themselves. Without a Giver, blessings cannot be acknowledged as gifts of love, and so there is no circle of love to be completed by the glad expression of thanks. A desire to find the Giver of the blessings of life in order to give thanks may not be a common path to faith, but it is a possible one. It probably happens most often when God shows his hand in unexpected occurrences that surprise people into wondering how or why they happened. They need not be miraculous in any strict sense, but they may be sufficiently out of the ordinary to surprise and provoke wonder. They may be coincidences that look too good to be merely accidental. Wonder and thanksgiving are closely related.

One way of recognizing the difference that thanksgiving to God makes is to see it as a movement from ourselves and our concerns toward God. Lives that may have been narrowly focused on our own concerns, and necessarily so in situations of significant need, are opened up to a wider perspective. The change in our circumstances that gives rise to thanksgiving will have been liberating, but thanksgiving takes that liberation

further. We are freed from the narrow perspectives that shut
out God and, with God, so much else. But thanksgiving is not
a movement from our own concerns to God that leaves them
behind, as pure contemplation of God's goodness may do. If it
is more than momentary, it is a process that continually moves
back and forth from our lives to God. It recognizes God in our
lives and opens our lives to God. Frequent thanksgiving, for
blessings large and small, is a way of living our lives with God.
The more we thank God, the more we adopt a habit of thanksgiving, the more open we become to the continuing grace of
God in our lives and the more sensitive we become to discern-
ing God's presence and activity in other lives and the world.

In petition and intercession we desire God's presence and
activity in situations of need, our own or those of others. In
thanksgiving we recognize God's presence and activity in our
own lives and the world. A life of prayer entails both. Thanksgiving emboldens us to ask for more. Intercession grows weari-
some without thanksgiving. Beyond both, there is a third form
of address to God: praise. Thanksgiving may lead to praise and
perhaps should lead to praise, but praise is a further step in the
orientation of our lives to God. We shall return to it.

In his poem "Gratefulness," George Herbert reflects on the
idea that, in addition to all the gifts of God for which we are
grateful, gratitude itself is a gift:

> Thou that hast given so much to me,
> Give one thing more, a grateful heart.[2]

The poem is a witty prayer in which he claims that, unless God
adds to all his gifts this additional one, "All thou hast given him

2. George Herbert, *The Country Parson, The Temple*, ed. John N. Wall, Classics of Western Spirituality (New York: Paulist Press, 1981), 245.

heretofore / is lost."[3] Without gratitude, the other gifts will not be received and enjoyed *as gifts*. Of course, Herbert could not be praying in this way if he did not already have some degree of gratitude, but he wants something more:

> Not thankful, when it pleaseth me;
> As if thy blessings had spare days:
> But such a heart, whose pulse may be
> Thy praise.[4]

The book of Psalms contains a variety of types of prayer or hymn. Among them, scholars commonly identify hymns of praise and songs of thanksgiving. The distinction between these two types is not absolute. They overlap. Praise and thanksgiving are closely related (e.g., Pss. 92:1; 100:4), and thanksgiving can be considered a type of praise. But the distinction is useful. Hymns of praise offer to God what is sometimes called "descriptive praise." God is praised for what he is and what he regularly and characteristically does—as Creator and ruler of the whole creation and as the covenant God who acts on behalf of his people. The songs of thanksgiving, on the other hand, focus on a specific and recent intervention of God to deliver either the community or an individual.

We shall focus here on the individual songs of thanksgiving because of their relevance to the personal story I have told in this book. They may also be called testimony psalms, because they presuppose a communal context (such as the temple) in which the psalmist gives thanks publicly and so bears witness to the community to the way God's power and love have been shown in the psalmist's deliverance from trouble. Good examples are Psalms 18, 30, 32, 34, 41, 92, 116, 118, 138. Each of

---

3. Herbert, *The Country Parson*, 245.
4. Herbert, *The Country Parson*, 246.

these has distinctive features, but there are also major common elements that suggest that these psalmists were guided by a pattern. It is worth remembering, when we read or study the Psalms, that the collection we have was formed as the hymn-book of the Jerusalem temple. Each psalm must have had a specific author or origin, but it proved suitable for regular use by the community or by individuals who could apply it to their own needs and circumstances. Some were doubtless written with the intention that they be hymns for regular use, but the songs of thanksgiving reflect an author's particular experience. In such cases, the particularity matched the similar experiences of other and later worshipers who expressed their own thanks in these words. People who pray the Psalms still read them in this way.

Each of the psalms of individual thanksgiving tells a concrete story of distress and deliverance by God. In that sense they are very personal. In them God is "my God" (Pss. 18:2; 30:12; 118:28). We cannot usually be sure what form of trouble the psalmist was in or what form the deliverance took. These things are expressed in more metaphorical than literal terms, which is what makes these psalms transferable from the experience of the psalmist to the experiences of those who later pray them.

There are some indications of serious illness (Pss. 32:3; 41:8), and rather characteristically these psalmists speak of being on the verge of death, plucked by God from the very jaws of the underworld (18:4–5; 30:3; 116:3, 8). There is also deliverance from enemies (18:17–18). Modern readers who want to pray these psalms for themselves may find these descriptions too extreme for application to their own less extreme circumstances, but it may be that some of these depictions were always hyperbolic and that ancient Jews praying these psalms were not by any means always close to death or surrounded by threatening enemies. Sudden diminishments of life, such as illness or deprivation, could be felt as falling into the power of death and being dragged down toward total loss of life. Like the "mighty waters" from which the Lord rescued one psalmist (Ps. 18:16) or "the desolate pit" and "the miry bog" from which he pulled another to safety (40:2), all these images can be treated as expressions of serious threats to well-being.

If the nature of the psalmists' distress is only vaguely depicted, the way in which they have been delivered by God is given hardly any literal depiction. God, we hear, "delivered me from all my fears" (Ps. 34:4). He "delivered my soul from death, my eyes from tears, my feet from stumbling" (116:8). He has protected the psalmist from enemies by means of his powerful right hand (138:7). Most notably, perhaps, the psalmist experienced a transformation of his condition, like the transformation of night into morning (30:5):

> You have turned my mourning into dancing;
>   you have taken off my sackcloth
>   and clothed me with joy. (Ps. 30:11)

God is recognized in this kind of life-changing intervention, and it's this that funds the psalmist's heartfelt and unstinting thanksgiving (30:12).

It is very important that, in addition to God's great acts of deliverance in the origins of the nation, focused on the exodus, the Psalms give a place to acts of deliverance in these little stories of individuals. The provision of these psalms for others to use shows that such experiences are not expected to be unusual. In such experiences God is found to be the same God who is proclaimed in the recitals of Israel's history. He is characterized by steadfast love and faithfulness (Pss. 32:10; 40:10; 92:2; 138:2). He is gracious, righteous, and merciful (116:5). In testifying to what they have experienced, the psalmists testify to others that this is indeed what the God of Israel is like and this is how he acts. Whereas in the hymns of praise God is praised for being who he is and for displaying these characteristics generally, in the songs of thanksgiving this is, so to speak, verified in the lives of individuals.

When a thanksgiving psalm was recited or sung in the temple, it would accompany a sacrifice, a thank offering (an animal along with cakes of bread; see Lev. 7:11–18). The sacrifice enhanced the giving of thanks. Both took place in public, among family and friends who would share in eating the sacrifice, and also in view of the crowd of worshipers in the temple (Ps. 116:17–19). As John Goldingay explains, "As usual sacrament and word accompany one another. . . . A verbal declaration of gratefulness without an expression of it that costs something would not be very impressive, but a concrete expression of gratefulness unaccompanied by interpretation would not give clear enough glory to [the Lord]."[5]

It is notable that, in Israel, there was a ritual for an individual to use in order to give thanks to God for their deliverance and as an act of witness to other members of the worshiping community (Ps. 66:13–16). There is no such provision in most Christian churches. At least in contemporary churches in the West, to my knowledge, people are not encouraged to declare to others what God has done for them in particular acts of blessing and restoration to well-being. In our worship we pray for the sick, but we do not give thanks for their recovery. The same goes for other forms of distress and suffering that people go through. In the Eucharist (which means "thanksgiving" in Greek), we regularly give thanks for what God has done for our salvation through Jesus's death and resurrection, just as Israel

5. John Goldingay, *Psalms*, vol. 3, *Psalms 90–150*, Baker Commentary on the Old Testament: Wisdom and Psalms (Grand Rapids: Baker Academic, 2008), 345.

celebrated the exodus and the other great acts of God in their history. In the baptism of adults there can be scope for those being baptized to testify to the way God has brought them to faith and salvation. Perhaps the Eucharist could also be a context for individuals to make their declarations of thanks for God's other remarkable interventions in their lives.

On the theme of the thank offering, there is a striking variation in Psalm 40:6. The psalmist declares that God desires not sacrifice but rather an ear receptive to God's commands (if that is the meaning of the obscure reference to the ear). Probably this is not as absolute a rejection of sacrifice as it sounds. As in the words of the prophet, "I desire steadfast love and not sacrifice" (Hosea 6:6), the meaning is that God is less concerned with sacrifice than with doing good. (First Samuel 15:22 puts the same contrast in an explicitly relative rather than absolute form.) Accordingly, the psalmist goes on to declare, "I delight to do your will, O my God; your law is within my heart" (Ps. 40:8). The suggestion is that gratitude and witness should be enacted by more than verbal and ritual acts. They should be lived out in a life all the more aligned with God's intentions.

In some of the psalms of thanksgiving, the psalmist declares the intention of continuing to thank God forever. Psalm 30 ends on such a note: "O LORD my God, I will give thanks to you forever" (30:12). The kind of life-saving deliverance this psalmist had experienced leads to a life characterized by thanksgiving. Although it is not spelled out, we can imagine that the psalmist will not only continue to thank God for this experience itself but will also, as a result of the experience, become more aware of God's goodness in all the blessings of life so that thankfulness becomes something like an attitude of mind, a way of relating to God all the time.

Psalm 34 begins with such a declaration, even before the psalmist goes on to tell the story of his deliverance:

> I will bless the LORD at all times;
>   his praise shall continually be in my mouth.
> My soul makes its boast in the LORD;
>   let the humble hear and be glad.
> O magnify the LORD with me,
>   and let us exalt his name together. (34:1–3)

Here the psalmist does not want his thanksgiving to stop with him. He wants others to join him in praising God, because the testimony he goes on to give will be good news for all who know their need of God. In fact, the psalm quickly moves from recounting the psalmist's own experience (34:4–6) to generalizing from it. Most of the psalm describes how God similarly looks after and rescues from danger all the righteous who fear him (34:7–10, 15–22). In this way, his own thanksgiving moves into praise and the invitation to others to praise God with him. Thanksgiving for his own deliverance on a specific occasion moves into praise to God for what he regularly does.

> When the righteous cry for help, the LORD hears,
>   and rescues them from all their troubles. (34:17)

His own experience has given him the confidence to invite others to "taste and see that the LORD is good" (34:8).

While these psalms offer us a vision of life lived in perpetual thanksgiving and praise, we know, of course, that thanksgiving is likely to be interrupted by further troubles. Goldingay provides a diagram of a circle on which he plots the sequence of moments of life with God that the various types of psalm express: Protest (or Lament)→ Plea (Petition)→ Trust→ Thanksgiving→ Obedience→ Praise→ Protest (or Lament)→ (and so on).

He says that this is really a spiral that one can enter at any point: "Understanding the movement as a spiral also recognizes that the next time a person sings a praise psalm, the words mean something different. Each time people go around the spiral, each element has more depth. The praise can be more nuanced. The protest can be more urgent. The trust can be deeper. The testimony can be more fervent."[6] This is helpful, but it is, of course, a scheme and so relates to real life only in an approximate way. For example, praise of God does not, even in the Psalms, arise only from such a sequence. As the psalms that feature creation and Israel's history show, we praise God also for the wonders of his creation and for his great acts of salvation for all of us in the biblical story.

There is also this question: What do we do when a plea for deliverance is not answered, at least not as we expect, and there seems not to be anything to give thanks for? Only the author of Psalm 88 seems to speak out of such a situation, and it is remarkable that this psalm of nearly despairing entreaty was included in the hymnbook of the temple. The only hope it offers is that the psalmist does continue to cry out to God. It was recognized in Israel that there would be people who would need this psalm, an anguished and so far unanswered cry from the depths.

It needs to be stressed that thanksgiving does not obliterate the memory of sadness, pain, and loss. It does not evince what Martin Luther called a "theology of glory" or what modern theologians sometimes call "triumphalism." In other words, however blessed and uplifted we may feel, we have not been

6. John Goldingay, *Psalms*, vol. 1, *Psalms 1–41*, Baker Commentary on the Old Testament: Wisdom and Psalms (Grand Rapids: Baker Academic, 2006), 68–69.

exalted out of this world of tears and troubles. We are still weak and vulnerable humans, subject to the common lot of this fallen world, sharing it with millions who live in grinding poverty or suffer all manner of diminishments of life. In a comfortable life, it is easy to forget such people, partly because of a failure of empathy, an inability to imagine the sufferings of others. Even if our own sufferings have been comparatively slight, remembering them is a step toward empathy and solidarity with others. As always, Jesus must be our example. The Letter to the Hebrews regards him as qualified to be our heavenly high priest because on earth he fully shared our human weakness and "offered up prayers and supplications, with loud cries and tears, to the one who was able to save him from death" (Heb. 5:7). Even in his exalted glory, Jesus has not forgotten the plight from which he was delivered by resurrection. He understands and cares about all who are afflicted.

Not long ago I met someone I have known for years, though I have been in contact with him only occasionally. I have always known that he had a rare kind of sight impairment that was bound to get worse. I have admired the way he has pursued a demanding career. But on this occasion, because of my own struggles with sight impairment, I had no hesitation in asking him much more about his condition. I felt for him more strongly, and I will try to go on praying for him.

On one occasion (probably one of many), the apostle Paul had a narrow escape from death (2 Cor. 1:9). We do not know any details, but it was shortly before he wrote his Second Letter to the Corinthians and seems to have strongly affected what he wrote in that letter. He begins the letter, following the opening greeting, with something like a psalm of thanksgiving, in which he refers to his deliverance as God "comforting" or "consoling" him, perhaps with reference to Isaiah 51:3, 12. Like the psalmists, he hopes that others will be able to share in his thanksgiving

(2 Cor. 1:11), but there is also a distinctive feature of his thanksgiving. He says that just as Jesus suffered so that he would be able to "comfort" others, so did Paul himself. (In this passage, "we" is an epistolary plural, functioning as "I.")

> Blessed be the God and Father of our Lord Jesus Christ, the Father of mercies and the God of all consolation, who consoles us in all our affliction, so that we may be able to console those who are in any affliction with the consolation with which we ourselves are consoled by God. For just as the sufferings of Christ are abundant for us, so also our consolation is abundant through Christ. If we are being afflicted, it is for your consolation and salvation; if we are being consoled, it is for your consolation, which you experience when you patiently endure the same sufferings that we are also suffering. (2 Cor. 1:3–6)

Paul's special consciousness of an apostolic ministry that gave him a very close and responsible relationship with the churches he founded is operative here, but the passage can still be instructive for us all. Affliction and "consolation" from God prepare us to empathize with and console others who are afflicted in similar or even very different ways. From Christ's solidarity with us in suffering on the cross, loving consolation flows to us and then overflows from us to others. Our thanksgiving, like Paul's, should encompass all this, and we should act on it. (I hope this book may help others experience God's consolation in their lives, as I have.)

When I think now of the loving consolation I received from God during the story I have told in this book, I think especially of the blurred cross. I recall when I sat in the chapel at Addenbrooke's Hospital, on the very worst day of this experience, and ahead of me was the black cross, "blurred" because that was how I saw it. It expressed the loving solidarity of the crucified Jesus with me. It had never occurred to me before that Jesus's own eyesight must have been blurred, cloudy with tears and blood, when he hung on the cross. As his cross was blurred to me, so his loving sight of me was blurred. It now strikes me as part of the meaning of that experience that the place was a chapel in a large and busy hospital. I had come from and would soon return to the eye clinic, where I would sit in the overflowing waiting room among the socially distanced chairs of other patients, silent, no doubt anxious about what degree of sight they could expect to have from then on. Some were waiting for treatment that would remedy or ameliorate their impairments. Others would learn there was nothing much that could be done. Their sight would go on degenerating. As I sat before the blurred cross, I was not isolated from them, and neither was the Christ who was symbolized by the cross. In medieval hospitals there were crucifixes or paintings of the passion in wards so that patients lying on their beds could be reminded of Christ's suffering for them and receive the consolation of his love. Nowadays nurses are not even permitted to ask patients if they would like them to pray for them.

Among Christians, it is the event and the symbol of the cross at the heart of our faith that makes it impossible to forget the afflicted. When Luther opposed a "theology of glory," he preferred in its stead a "theology of the cross." We meet God most profoundly in affliction, his and ours.

In a sequence of 150 poems he calls "Psalter," the poet Micheal O'Siadhail writes poems addressed to God, inspired to some extent by the biblical psalms. They are personal and moving, embodying O'Siadhail's intense and day-by-day experience of God. A striking characteristic of them is how frequently they sound a note of thanksgiving and praise. O'Siadhail is a man who delights in life, and he cannot stop thanking God for everything that delights him. Indeed, thanksgiving is integral to the delight. He experiences life in a way that cannot but give rise to praise.

One poem, all about thanksgiving, is somewhat comparable with George Herbert's "Gratefulness." Like Herbert, O'Siadhail surprises readers with a poetic conceit: the notion that he has to apologize to God for the tedious way he is constantly repeating his thanks:

> Forgive me how I must repeat myself—
> Every day I live
> I say my prayer of thanks.

He cannot help his overflowing gratitude for the "way you've lavished love on me." He is a lover, so in love he must as "any lover does repeat myself."[7]

In another poem he reflects on the prospects and perils of old age. Since he is about the same age as I am, I feel some affinity with this poem. He prays,

> Though I will take what extent you assign,
> Please let me keep praising line after line,
> Please let me love more before I must leave.

In the last stanza he asks that he may be able, even in a frail and dependent condition,

> Still to rejoice, never just to resign;
> Grateful for what all this time has been mine,
> Let me then go, giving thanks to the end.[8]

7. O'Siadhail, *Testament*, 63. This is "psalm" 60 of his "Psalter."
8. O'Siadhail, *Testament*, 98. This is "psalm" 94 of his "Psalter."

In chapter 1, I quoted T. S. Eliot's famous line: "Old men ought to be explorers." I should like to add another proposal: "The old should be thanksgivers." One of the tasks and joys of old age should be to look back over the whole course of one's life and remember it with thanksgiving to God. As O'Siadhail suggests in the lines quoted at the beginning of this chapter, no experience is really owned until we give thanks for it. Similarly, I suggest, no life is complete, insofar as it can ever be completed, without gratitude and thanksgiving to God.

To say that an old person is someone with a long life behind them is mere tautology. But in the quest to stay young and feel young, some of my contemporaries try not to think about that. Yet it is the wonder of being old. At least until memory fails, it is the advantage the old have over younger people, an advantage that counterbalances the obvious disadvantages of being old. It is the source of the distinctive contributions the old can make to the common life and even pass on to later generations. Some old people claim not to recognize the "I" of their early memories as the same self they feel themselves to be now. It is certainly a feature of childhood memories that we do not seem able to "get inside" them as we can the memories of later years. It is also the case that our younger selves, in memories we can still experience as subjects, can seem embarrassingly or shamefully different from the selves we have become. All the same, we need to own them, just as we have to agree that it is we who are portrayed in early photographs, even though we might not be able to identify ourselves without help from others. It is a matter of personal integrity and responsibility to own the whole extent of our lives. Even if I have changed quite radically, through conversion or reform, through a radical change of heart or direction, or through some tragically life-changing experience, all that I have been still contributes in some way to who I have become. We need to own it all.

Of course, we do not remember everything, not even everything important. But we should do our best not to edit our stories to our advantage, tempting though that is. Before God at least it is a futile exercise. Better to face up to what God knows anyway. But can we be thankful for everything? For God's part in it all, we can, for God has intended nothing but our good. The advantage of the vantage point that old age gives us is that we can see that we were often wrong about what we thought was good for us. We can see how what turned out was really better for us than what we wanted. We can also see how God brought good out of things that went wrong, whether through our own foolishness or fault or otherwise. Undoubtedly things did go wrong, often seriously wrong, but by God's grace the outcomes were better than they might have been. If that is not always the case, it is probably true more often than we recognize. God redeems our sins by making less of them than they had the potential to be, just as he enhances the good things we do by making more of them than we could do ourselves. All this is involved in tracing the hand of God in our lives and adding the seal of thankfulness and thanksgiving to all these experiences. Just as distance may put them in a new perspective, so thanksgiving can enhance them, as in memory, reflection, and thanksgiving we experience a further dimension of them.

There are things in our past, perhaps even whole tracts, for which we cannot be thankful. We cannot thank God for our own willful evil. We may be grateful for the ways in which he brought some good out of these events, but not for our evil intentions and actions. I am not as sure as many Christian counselors that all memories can be healed in this life. We can be assured of God's forgiveness, but it may be good for us for a process of repentance and regret to continue. We have to live with the seriousness of what we have done. To say, as one often hears now, that God has forgiven us and so we must forgive ourselves is simplistic. As Christians in earlier times knew, there may be works of repentance to be done, not because God's forgiveness is conditional but because the perfecting of our moral character is not a matter of instant transformation. We need to avoid the moral shallowness and carelessness of our culture. Forgiving others is a clear duty, but forgiving ourselves is more complex. It may involve those we have hurt or destroyed, and it may become fully possible only after death. There is also all the harm we have done without, in our moral insensitivity and carelessness, realizing it.

So we cannot be thankful for everything we have done. But our lives are woven out of God's providence and our free will. Our thankfulness to God for his role, an overriding part that allows us our freedom within limits, should mature as we age and look back with greater wisdom and a fuller attunement to God's purposes. What of our achievements, the things of which we can be proud? Modern people may instinctively feel that being grateful for them undermines our own self-worth and justified pride. But anyone who reflects on their achievements knows that they were not possible without circumstances and people who helped to make them possible. When someone appears on a stage to receive a medal for a major achievement and they thank all the people who contributed to their ability to achieve, they usually do so gladly and gratefully. The pleasure of achieving is enhanced, not diminished, by sharing credit with others. Some people labor alone against the odds in unfavorable circumstances, but even they are not "self-made" people. Something, perhaps genetics, perhaps early experiences, perhaps some influential figure in their past, or perhaps a personal hero who inspires them (and there are other possibilities), made them people who could do that, whereas others could not have done. In short, we do not minimize real achievements by recognizing dependence. Thanking God for making our achievements possible enhances their value, just as gratitude always does. We are glad to have done them, recognizing them as the gifts of God's love to us and through us to others.

"The old should be thanksgivers." Surely thanksgiving is part of our calling, a reason why we have been spared to live as long as we have. It may lead us to other good things, such as generosity. It may lead us deeper into God's love, which is what Eliot intended with the image of exploration. It could be the last we can do, as we echo O'Siadhail's prayer:

> Grateful for what all this time has been mine,
> Let me then go, giving thanks to the end.[9]

---

9. O'Siadhail, *Testament*, 98. This is "psalm" 94 of his "Psalter."

Scripture Index

About the Author

Richard Bauckham is a biblical scholar, theologian, and poet. Born in 1946, he grew up in north London and studied at the University of Cambridge, where his BA and PhD were both in history. He taught historical and contemporary theology at the University of Manchester for fifteen years and then was Professor of New Testament Studies at the University of St. Andrews, Scotland, for fifteen years. He now lives in Cambridge and frequently visits St. Andrews. Among his many books, the best known are probably *Jesus and the Eyewitnesses: The Gospels as Eyewitness Testimony* (2006, expanded edition 2017), *God Crucified: Monotheism and Christology in the New Testament* (1998), *The Theology of the Book of Revelation* (1993), *The Bible and Ecology: Rediscovering the Community of Creation* (2010), *Jesus: A Very Short Introduction* (2011), and *Who Is God? Key Moments of Biblical Revelation* (2020). Never able to confine his interests to a narrow field, he has also written about the theology of Jürgen Moltmann, the Gospel of John, the letters of James, Jude and 2 Peter, eschatology, women in the Gospels, early Judaism, apocryphal Christian literature, and Old Testament pseudepigrapha, among other topics. He has written some poetry throughout his adult life, but in the last decade it has become an important part of his life and writing. He is an Anglican layman who sometimes preaches. He is a Fellow of the British Academy and a Fellow of the Royal Society of Edinburgh. He has traveled widely, giving invited lectures in the US, Japan, Ethiopia, Australia, New Zealand, Italy, France, South Korea, Taiwan, Canada, and other countries. Some of his heroes are Francis of Assisi, Vincent van Gogh, Helen Waddell, Jürgen Moltmann, Siegfried Sassoon, and the characters in Tove Jansson's Moomin books. He enjoys gardens, historic places of all kinds, cakes, novels, good drama, and not-too-strenuous walks. After the events described in this book, he still has many ongoing writing projects. He hopes, when he gets older, to have a cat. There is further information on his website: www.richardbauckham.co.uk.